GREAT ITALIAN COOKING

Valerie A. Dominioni

Doubleday & Company, Inc.
Garden City, New York
1987

Dedication

This book is dedicated to my husband Angelo and my
daughter Silvana, who tasted every recipe in this
book at least once!

Library of Congress Cataloging-in-Publication Data

Dominioni, Valerie Ann, 1944–
  Great Italian cooking.

  Includes index.
  1. Cookery, Italian.   I. Title.
TX723.D66   1987   641.5945   86–19807
ISBN 0–385–23972–6

Produced by Smallwood & Stewart, 156 Fifth Avenue,
New York, New York 10010
First edition
Printed in Singapore

TABLE OF CONTENTS

About the Author

Valerie A. Dominioni graduated Phi Beta Kappa from Hunter College in 1965 and received her Master of Arts Degree from Cornell University in 1967. Active in the Italian food industry, Ms. Dominioni has had the opportunity to learn first hand about Italian cheeses and the cuisine of Italy.

Because there is so little information on how to serve and enjoy the cheeses of Italy, Valerie decided to write a comprehensive book on these magnificent cheeses for the American consumer. The author has combined her training and life-long interest in Italy to create a book which is truly of interest and value to her fellow Americans.

Dear Reader,

I have written this book to make the average person aware of the quality, variety and versatility of Italian cheeses.

One of the most important differences between the Italian and American way of eating is the prominent position that cheese has in the Italian diet. In Italy, cheese is an integral part of the meal and is used as a basic cooking ingredient. A versatile food, cheese is used in sauces, soups, pasta and rice dishes, meat entrees and desserts.

In recent years a great many specialty cheeses have been imported into the United States and consumers have become increasingly more adventurous in experimenting with new cheeses. As with all things new and unfamiliar, however, the consumer needs relevant information in regard to buying, serving and storing these products.

Like many people, I have often had the experience of being in a supermarket or specialty store confronted by a multitude of products and overwhelmed by the sheer number of items. Not knowing the difference between one product and another, I either bought on impulse or I stuck to the old, tried and familiar.

On one such occasion, while I was trying in vain to identify a group of unlabeled "gourmet" vegetables in the produce section, I happened to glance over at the cheese section where I saw more than fifty varieties of cheese piled in a large bin. I wondered whether the people buying cheese were doing so in the same hit-or-miss fashion as I bought unfamiliar products. I found out that they did. It was then I decided that there was a definite need for a book on Italian cheese — one which would describe in detail the unique flavor, texture and body of these exquisite cheeses along with practical advice on buying, serving and storing them. I wanted to include the background and history of individual Italian cheeses as well. Each variety of cheese has a tradition of its own and is often the result of centuries of experience. Because we Americans have become so nutrition-conscious in recent years, I also wanted to include nutritional information for each of the cheeses discussed in detail. Finally, I wanted to collect recipes from all regions of Italy which would best show how these cheeses are used.

The recipes in this book are authentic Italian recipes which come from northern, southern and central Italy. Italy is divided into nearly twenty geographical regions and each of these regions has its own characteristic cuisine. The cheese recipes in this book reflect the individual cuisines of Italy.

Our recipes are for all occasions — special meals for "company," casual get-togethers, everyday meals, picnics, "covered dish" parties, after-school snacks, light lunches. The versatility of Italian cheeses will astound and delight you!

Simple and straightforward, these recipes, with very few exceptions, are easy to prepare. They are very flexible and fit easily into the framework of a traditional American meal.

The American vs. the Italian Way of Eating

The Italian way of eating is quite different from that of the United States. The meals themselves and the time of the day at which they are eaten differ markedly. While breakfast is considered an important and substantial meal in the United States, it is not so in Italy. The morning meal is a very light affair — just a roll and coffee, i.e., a "continental breakfast" — no eggs and bacon, cereal and fruit, or pancakes with breakfast sausage.

On the other hand, our lunch, consisting of a sandwich and beverage, is light compared to the Italian midday meal which is their main meal of the day. At 1:00-1:30 people leave work to eat the main meal of the day, which lasts between one and one and a half hours. The traditional Italian dinner follows the menu below:

(Appetizer)
First Course of Soup, Rice or Pasta
Second Course of Fish, Meat or Poultry
Side Dish of Vegetables
Salad
Fruit or Cheese
Sweets, (if any)
Coffee

The midday meal has become more simple in recent years but it is still more substantial than our lunch.

The Italian workday ends at 7:00-7:30 and the evening meal is generally eaten between 7:30 and 8:00 p.m. It is much lighter than the midday meal and corresponds more closely to our lunch. At this meal Italians may have a first course of soup, followed by a serving of meat, or they may eat an omelette, a cheese and vegetable dish, or a cold meat platter. The meal almost invariably ends with a serving of fresh fruit.

Because Italian and American eating habits are so different, I have not tried to recreate an Italian meal from start to finish but rather to adapt these Italian dishes to the American way of eating.

In this introductory section, I have included sample menus which feature at least one cheese dish per meal. I have made an attempt to blend these dishes in with the traditional American meal. I believe you will truly enjoy these cheese recipes and discover for yourself the versatility and flavor of the magnificent cheeses from Italy.

Sincerely,

Valerie J. Donzelli

INTRODUCTION

Cheese and Today's Consumer

Our purpose in writing this book is to show the versatility of Italian cheese. We wish to dispel the notion that cheese can *only* be enjoyed by itself on a cheese tray, on a slice of bread or on top of spaghetti. Italian cheese can be served in combination with meat, fish, vegetables, rice, pasta, fruit or nuts.

Before cooking with cheese, however, we must first know how to buy it. Seeing a bin full of cheese in a supermarket or a cheese display case in a specialty shop can overwhelm a consumer who asks himself:

1. What kind of cheese is this?
2. How is it different from other types of cheese displayed with it?
3. Is this cheese mild or sharp in taste?
4. How do I know that this cheese is fresh?
5. How do I serve this cheese?
6. How do I store this cheese?
7. How long will it stay fresh?
8. Will the flavor change with storage?
9. Can I freeze it?
10. How much cheese should I buy at one time?
11. What other foods can I serve with it?

To answer these questions, we will discuss buying, storing, and handling of cheese in general, followed by a more detailed description of the cheeses which we feel are most representative of Italy.

ITALY
A Tradition of Cheese Making

Italy is one of the greatest producers of cheese in the world. Some Italian cheeses, such as Pecorino Romano and Caciocavallo, date back to ancient Rome while Fontina, Gorgonzola, Parmigiano, Grana Padano and Taleggio have their origins in the Middle Ages. Not content to rest on her laurels, Italy has continued to make contributions to cheese-making in modern times with the development of Bel Paese® in the early 1900's and, most recently, of *Torte di Formaggio*, layered cheese "cakes."

Italy makes cheese not only from cow's milk, but from sheep's and goat's milk and from the milk of the water buffalo as well. Indeed, this beautiful country makes cheese from a combination of these different types of milk.

Italian cheeses vary greatly in texture. At one end of the spectrum is Mascarpone, a highly perishable, fresh cheese with the texture of thick whipped cream. At the other end is the granular, closely textured Parmigiano-Reggiano with a shelf life* of two years or longer. In between these two extremes are soft, semi-soft, semi-hard and hard cheeses whose shelf life varies from two to twelve months.

There is an Italian cheese for all tastes ranging from the mild to tangy to piquant. You will find an Italian cheese for each course of the meal whether it be the appetizer, first course, main course, or dessert.

The quality of Italian cheese is jealously guarded by individual Consortia of Italian Cheesemakers. These non-profit organizations establish standards and characteristics for their respective cheeses and oversee their production to make sure that these standards are met.

There are hundreds of varieties of Italian cheeses, most of which never leave Italy. The kind of milk selected, the type of rennet used to curdle the milk, the temperature at which the milk is heated, the way the curd is treated, what cultures are added, how much moisture the cheese contains and how long the cheese is ripened will all determine what kind of cheese will result.

*The time that a product retains its freshness.

Cheese Storage Room the "Cathedral"

Preparing the Cheese Cloth

Drawing Out the Curd

Cheese and Nutrition

Cheese is a nutritious food — an excellent source of high-quality protein, calcium, riboflavin, phosphorus and vitamin A. Three ounces of Parmigiano-Reggiano, for instance, supply more protein than the same amount of beef, chicken or fish.[1]

Dairy products form one of the four basic food groups, and nutritionists urge that some milk products be eaten every day in order to satisfy nutritional needs.[2] In fact, dental researchers at the University of Minnesota have found out that eating cheese can actually prevent tooth decay. According to Dr. Charles Schachtele, Professor of Dentistry and Microbiology, cavity-causing bacteria form and thrive in the acid layer which forms on the teeth when food is eaten. Cheese, however, prevents foods from forming this acid layer on the teeth and therefore, prevents cavities from developing.[3]

Since a proper diet is a concern to us all, we have included nutritional information about the cheeses included in this cookbook.

Cheese is often cited as a food high in fat. I have often been asked the question, "If you eat so much cheese, why aren't you fat?" The answer is simple. Cheese, as all foods, must be eaten in moderation within the context of a balanced diet. Even a cheese with a high-fat content may still be eaten within a low-fat diet. Gorgonzola, for instance, contains 8.5 grams of fat in a one-ounce serving. Two to three ounces can be eaten and still be within the limit of 50 grams of fat of a low-fat diet.[4] We do suggest, however, that you consult with your physician regarding the advisability of eating a particular cheese if you have been put upon a strict diet.

All the cheeses referred to in this book contain sodium. The nutritional tables following the individual descriptions of each cheese should be read if you are on a low-sodium diet.

[1] Arnold E. Bender, *Dictionary of Nutrition and Food Technology* (Chemical Publishing Co., Inc. New York, 1976.)

[2] Hansen, Wyse, Sorenson, *Nutritional Quality Index of Foods* (AVI Publishing Co., Inc. Westport, CT) p. 67.

[3] Schachtele, Charles F., and Harlauder, Susan K. "Will the Diets of the Future Be Less Cariogenic?" Symposium 25, *Journal of Canadian Dental Assoc.*, No. 3, 1984, pp. 213-218.

[4] *Encyclopedia Brittanica, Volume 13, Macropedia* (Encyclopedia Brittanica Inc. Chicago/Toronto 1978) 15th Edition pp. 424-425.

Text article states that while the average daily fat intake is 100 grams of fat, the recommended intake is 78 grams of fat per day. A low-fat diet, on the other hand, includes 50 grams of fat per day.

Left, cheese past its prime. Right, cheese at its peak of flavor.

Flavor and Freshness in Italian Cheese

Each type of cheese, as we have said, has its own "shelf life." In general, the fresher a cheese is — i.e., the less time it is cured — and the softer a cheese is — i.e., the more moisture it contains — the shorter its life span will be. Conversely, the harder a cheese is, the less moisture it contains, the longer it will maintain its flavor.

Mascarpone, a fresh, cream cheese, normally has a shelf life of up to ten days. Bel Paese®, with less moisture and a curing time of fifty days, has a shelf life of three to four months, while Grana Padano, with an average curing time of up to eighteen months, has a shelf life of one to one and a half years.

The problem the consumer faces, however, is that he or she does not know how long the cheese may have been in the retailer's refrigerated unit or in a warehouse before bringing it home.

There are, however, certain taste characteristics that a cheese past its prime will have, and these will be an aid in detecting cheese no longer at its peak of flavor.

A fresh cheese like Mascarpone will develop an off taste which is slightly sour. Bel Paese®, Taleggio and other semi-soft cheeses will be acid in taste. Gorgonzola, spotted with obvious gray and pink discolorations, will develop a mouth-curdling acidity. Fontina will become pungent, losing its delicate nuttiness. An old Parmigiano-Reggiano or Grana Padano will become very dry and develop a stale flavor. Pecorino Romano and Provolone will develop an eye-watering pungency.

If you can, try to taste the cheese before buying it. However, if the cheese is prewrapped, taste it when you get home and return it to the retailer if you believe it is an old cheese.

Buying and Storing Natural Cheeses

An average portion of cheese is one to two ounces depending upon the richness or piquancy of the cheese. The more pronounced the cheese's flavor, the smaller the portion should be. If the cheese is somewhat perishable, buy what you think you will use within a short time. If a cheese appears to be "sweating" or if there is any discoloration, do not buy it.

Natural cheese is a living food and will continue to ripen in your refrigerator, becoming more pronounced in taste.

While all cheeses differ from one another in important ways, there are some general rules which may be applied to all cured cheeses.

1. Store all cheeses under refrigeration.
2. Serve cheese at room temperature (65°-75°), removing it from the refrigerator at least one half hour before serving. (Fresh cream cheese, however, such as Mascarpone, should be served cold.)
3. Clean your knife or cheese wire before cutting different varieties of cheese so that the flavor of one cheese will not be picked up by another.
4. Wrap the cheese tightly in plastic wrap or aluminum foil to keep out as much moisture as possible to keep mold from developing.
5. Trim away mold if it does develop and rewrap cheese in clean paper.
6. Store individual types of cheeses in separate wraps because natural cheeses will absorb flavors and aromas of other cheeses.

We have experimented with freezing cheeses and feel that cheese definitely suffers from being frozen. The cheese separates into watery and solid parts and what was once joined in perfect harmony, is torn asunder.

The softer cheeses become watery and develop water either on the surface or within the body, losing their creamy consistencies. The harder cheeses, as Parmigiano-Reggiano and Grana Padano, develop a chalky look and dry taste. Mozzarella was the only cheese which did not suffer adversely from freezing.

If you should have to freeze cheese, use it for cooking rather than eating and do so at the earliest possible time.

THE CHEESES OF ITALY

The Cheeses of Italy

1. Parmigiano-Reggiano
2. Grana Padano
3. Pecorino Romano
4. Italico/Bel Paese®
5. Sheep's Milk
   Table Cheese
6. Caciotta
7. Mascarpone
8. Toscanello
9. Gorgonzola
10. Mozzarella
11. Fontina/Fontal
12. Provolone

Following are descriptions of the major Italian cheeses imported into the United States which are used as table cheeses and in cooking. After each description is a listing of the nutritional content of each cheese.

Bel Paese®

Bel Paese® (Bell Pie Aý Zay) brand of semi-soft cheese is Italy's most renowned table cheese. Bel Paese® is an Italico cheese — ivory in color and delicate in taste. Served most often with fresh fruit and crackers, Bel Paese® is also an excellent cooking cheese because its rich, buttery texture enables it to melt evenly and smoothly. Its mild taste enhances but does not overpower the many foods with which it is combined. This cheese adds a different dimension to eggs, vegetables, meats, pasta and fresh salads.

"Bel Paese" means 'beautiful country' — a phrase that Italians immediately identify with Italy. Italy's greatest poet, Dante Alighieri, first described the country that the "Appenine Mountains divide and the Alps and Sea surround" as *il bel paese*.

It was Antonio Stoppani, however, a well-traveled abbot, who named his book about Italy's natural beauties *Il Bel Paese*. Father Stoppani was a good friend of the cheesemaker Egidio Galbani's father. When Signor Galbani was looking for a name for the new cheese he had just created, he remembered the title of the abbot's monumental work. He asked the Stoppani family if he could name his new cheese Bel Paese®. The family happily agreed, but in return wanted his picture to appear on the label. Thus, the face you see on the label of the Bel Paese® semi-soft cheese is that of Father Stoppani.

Bel Paese® is made in Melzo, a little town south of Milan by the Egidio Galbani Company, one of Italy's largest manufacturers of cheese and pork products. It is made from cow's milk and cured for at least seven weeks.

Bel Paese®

As with all natural cheeses, Bel Paese® will continue to ripen in your refrigerator. The flavor of the cheese will become more pronounced as the cheese continues to ripen. Of course, being mild, Bel Paese® will never become overpowering. It can be kept safely under refrigeration for three to four months without becoming bitter and acid-tasting.

Wrap the cheese in either tight-fitting plastic wrap or in aluminum foil to prevent moisture from developing and settling under the wrap, facilitating the growth of mold. If moisture does form and mold develops, simply trim the mold away and wrap in a clean piece of plastic wrap.

I find that a cheese wire is the most efficient way of slicing Bel Paese® or any semi-soft cheese because it slices cleanly and evenly. You can, of course, use a knife blade. After removing the wax coating on the cheese, the white crust under the wax coating should also be removed because it tends to be moist and bitter-tasting.

Bel Paese brand of semi-soft cheese is a versatile cheese. It can be enjoyed as a table cheese with any type of bread or crackers or with fresh pears, apples or dark grapes. The cheese should be served at room temperature to bring out its full flavor. Remove it from the refrigerator at least one half hour before serving.

Bel Paese® is marvelous for cooking and our recipes run the gamut from hors d'oeuvres to main dishes. Bel Paese® is truly "a cheese for all seasons."

When you shop for Bel Paese®, you may see three different cheeses with the same trademark.

1. Imported Bel Paese® from Italy.
2. Domestic Bel Paese® manufactured in the United States.
3. Bel Paese® Medallion Process Cheese.

The original Bel Paese® is made in Italy and is the cheese with the map of Italy pictured on the label. FORMAGGIO BEL PAESE® is printed in green on the wax which covers the cheese with the Galbani logo in red.

Bel Paese®, manufactured here in the United States, has the map of North and South America on its label. The American version has the same creamy taste of the original, but it is milder in taste and somewhat paler in color.

Bel Paese® Medallion Cheese is process cheese, available in ¾-oz. rounds wrapped in gold foil bearing the map of Italy. Bel Paese® Medallion is an unusually creamy process cheese made from Bel Paese®, milk, cream and whey. This cheese has gained tremendous popularity here in the United States because of its convenience as a nutritious snacking and sandwich cheese. It may be used in cooking as well as in sauces and soups.

Nutritional Content
Per One-Ounce (28 grams) Serving

BEL PAESE®		BEL PAESE® MEDALLION	
Calories	90	Calories	71
Protein	5.74 g	Protein	3.36 g
Carbohydrates	.31 g	Carbohydrates	1.26 g
Fat	7.36 g	Fat	5.88 g
Calcium	165 mg	Calcium	106 mg
Iron	---	Iron	.08 mg
Vitamin A	87 µg*	Vitamin A	104 µg*
B_1 (Thiamine)	.002 mg	B_1 (Thiamine)	.006 mg
B_2 (Riboflavin)	.08 mg	B_2 (Riboflavin)	.08 mg
Niacin	.08 mg	Niacin	.03 mg
Sodium	196 mg	Sodium	193 mg

*µg = microgram, 1/1000 of a milligram.

Gorgonzola — the Creamy Blue

Gorgonzola (Gōr gōn zō´ lah) is an exquisite blue-mold cheese and is considered one of the finest cheeses in the world. It is the softest and most spreadable of the blue cheeses and though robust in flavor, is mild for a blue cheese.

Gorgonzola gets its name from the town of the same name located ten miles northeast from Milan, where it was first made in the ninth century. Hundreds of years ago when the cows returned from their pasture in the Alps, the town of Gorgonzola was the first resting place along the way. There the cows were milked and cheese was made. The cheeses produced from the milk of these tired (stracche) cows were called Stracchino. Gorgonzola is the most widely known of the cheeses that belong to the Stracchino family which were originally made at the end of the summer. (Taleggio also belongs to this group of cheeses.)

The Gorgonzola of today is still made in the cities of Lombardy and Piedmont. The cheese is made from whole cow's milk although in times past, Gorgonzola was also made from a mixture of cow's and goat's milk. It is cured for two to three months. The body of the cheese is ivory-colored with blue-green veining and its wrinkled crust is grayish-gold or reddish-brown in color.

Gorgonzola is a magnificent table cheese that can be eaten with crusty Italian or French bread, crackers or coarse-grained breads such as pumpernickel, rye, whole wheat or even oatmeal bread. We find it delicious on plain or onion bagels. A one-ounce serving of cheese is an average portion.

Serve Gorgonzola at room temperature, taking out the desired amount of cheese at least one half hour before serving. Cut it with a cheese wire or special cheese knife with a serrated edge.

Crisp vegetables, such as celery, as well as sweet pears and apples complement the cheese. A full-bodied red wine such as Barolo or Valpolicella goes well with Gorgonzola. If you prefer not to have wine with cheese, a strong iced tea which is not too sweet is a good accompaniment because it neither competes with nor is overwhelmed by the cheese's flavor.

Gorgonzola must always be kept under refrigeration and should be tightly wrapped in aluminum foil or in clear, tightly fitting plastic wrap. It is a very perishable cheese which can be stored up to a maximum of forty-five days under refrigeration. The longer the cheese is kept, the softer the body of the cheese will become and the more flavorful the taste. You may have to experiment with Gorgonzola to see at which point of maturity you like the cheese best. If you see that the body of the cheese is brown or pinkish in color, the cheese is overripe and should not be eaten.

Gorgonzola Dolcelatte™ (Gōr gōn zō´ lah Dól chay láh tay) is an especially creamy and sweet Gorgonzola, made by adding a laboratory-prepared mold and curdling agents to the milk. It is easier to digest and is more delicate in flavor than the traditional Gorgonzola. While Gorgonzola is most usually served as a table cheese, it is used frequently in combination with milk and cream to form sauces, and in pasta or rice dishes. It also is used with mascarpone and ricotta to make hors d'oeuvres.

We have included some recipes which use Gorgonzola in pizza, pasta, rice and main dishes as well.

Nutritional Content Per One-Ounce (28 grams) Serving			
GORGONZOLA			
Calories	93	B_1 (Thiamine)	.003 mg
Protein	5.38 g	B_2 (Riboflavin)	.05 mg
Carbohydrates	.06 g	Niacin	.25 mg
Fat	8.5 g[1]	Sodium	192 mg
Calcium	99 mg		
Iron	.08 mg		
Vitamin A	118 μg*		

[1]Gorgonzola Dolcelatte™ has 7.87 grams of fat per 28-gram serving.

*μg = microgram, 1/1000 of a milligram.

Parmigiano-Reggiano

Parmigiano-Reggiano (Par mē jáh no Redge áh no) has been called a true aristocrat . . . the absolute king of cured cheeses. As such, it has been served as a gourmet cheese for centuries.

As with many Italian cheeses Parmigiano-Reggiano dates back to the Middle Ages. After seven centuries the cheese is still made according to the same formula using completely natural ingredients. Parmigiano is made exclusively from the milk of cows within a carefully defined region in Italy — the Zona Tipica. (This geographical designation comprises the province of Parma, Reggio Emilia, Modena, Bologna on the left bank of the Reno River and Mantua on the right bank of the river Po.) The cheese is produced only from April to November.

Parmigiano-Reggiano should not be confused with its pale white imitation which is often found on supermarket shelves. The true Parmigiano is a unique cheese of unsurpassed flavor which is enjoyed as a table cheese and as a fundamental ingredient in Italian cuisine. It is used in soups, rice dishes, as in the famous *risotto,* meat dishes, sauces, and, of course, freshly grated on pasta.

It is no accident that its flavor is unsurpassable for the cheese is matured with the utmost care for *at least* two years. You will find the year in which the cheese was produced branded on the rind of the cheese. Highest in protein of all Italian cheeses, three ounces of Parmigiano-Reggiano supplies more protein than the same amount of beef, chicken or fish. In addition, it only takes one half hour to digest that portion of Parmigiano while it takes four hours to digest the meat.

Buy Parmigiano-Reggiano in chunks or wedges so that you can freshly grate whatever you need. The cheese can be kept in your refrigerator for more than one year. It must be wrapped well — either in aluminum foil or in tight-fitting plastic wrap. Do not grate large amounts of Parmigiano at one time because the cheese will develop mold due to its high moisture content. It is best to grate one half to one cup of cheese at a time and store in an air-tight plastic container for a few days only.

The cheese should be straw yellow or golden in color and have a granular texture. The true Parmigiano is marked from top to bottom all the way around with the words PARMIGIANO REGGIANO indelibly printed on the rind. This lettering is visible even on small portions so that you will be sure you are buying genuine Italian Parmigiano.

Nutritional Content Per One-Ounce (28 grams) Serving	
PARMIGIANO-REGGIANO	
Calories	105
Protein	10.08 g
Carbohydrates	---
Fat	7.14 g
Calcium	361 mg
Iron	.22 mg
Vitamin A	80 µg*
B_1 (Thiamine)	.006 mg
B_2 (Riboflavin)	.03 mg
Niacin	.03 mg
Sodium	188 mg

*µg = microgram, 1/1000 of a milligram.

Grana Padano

Northern Italy

Grana Padano (Gráh nah Pah dáh no) is a magnificent cheese which belongs to the same family of cheeses as Parmigiano-Reggiano.

The word Grana refers to the cheese's granular appearance while the word Padano means "of the Po." Grana Padano is manufactured all year-round in the Po Valley. The spring production is considered to be the better one by connoisseurs who differentiate between the two productions as Vernengo (from Inverno [*winter*]) and Maggengo (from Maggio [*May*]). The cheese is cured for fifteen to twenty-four months.

Grana Padano is white to straw-colored. Its creamy, savory taste makes it a superb table cheese which can be enjoyed with fruit, bread or all by itself. As Parmigiano, grated Grana Padano is sprinkled on soups and over pasta and is used in many recipes.

Although there are differences between Parmigiano and Grana Padano, both cheeses are superb and can be substituted for one another in our recipes. We do feel, however, that Parmigiano is superior as a table cheese.

Buy Grana Padano, as you would Parmigiano, in chunks or wedges and store tightly wrapped in foil or clear plastic wrap under refrigeration. The cheese stays fresh for at least one year. Freshly grate whatever you need and store any leftovers in a tightly sealed container.

Nutritional Content Per One-Ounce (28 grams) Serving	
GRANA PADANO	
Calories	105
Protein	10.08 g
Carbohydrates	---
Fat	7.14 g
Calcium	361 mg
Iron	.22 mg
Vitamin A	80 μg*
B_1 (Thiamine)	.006 mg
B_2 (Riboflavin)	.03 mg
Niacin	.03 mg
Sodium	188 mg

*μg = microgram, 1/1000 of a milligram.

Pecorino Romano

Pecorino Romano (Peck ō rē´ no Rō máh no) is an outstanding cheese made from sheep's milk. The cheese dates back to ancient Roman times when it was made for both domestic consumption and for shipment overseas. It remains today an integral part of central and southern Italian cuisine. Pecorino Romano is also extremely popular among Americans as the United States imports over 50% of the Romano produced in Italy — a demonstrative endorsement of this fabulous cheese.

Pecorino Romano has a sharp, piquant flavor. The cheese is made from whole sheep's milk curdled with lamb's rennet and is cured for at least eight months.

Pecorino Romano is an excellent grating cheese and, as such, is used in many pasta, meat and soup dishes. As a table cheese, Pecorino Romano is delicious with crusty Italian bread and a robust red wine. Since it is piquant, small portions are in order.

Although Pecorino Romano is still made in Latium, the area surrounding Rome, the major production of Romano is now situated in Sardinia where it has been since the early 1900's.

In Sardinia both industrial manufacture and farm production of Pecorino exist side by side. Both factory-made and shepherd-made Pecorino Romano are made according to traditional methods, but the two types of cheese reflect their respective ways of manufacture. The industrial Pecorino is uniform in shape, in size and flavor. The Pecorino made by the shepherds is naturally more individual in shape and size as it is made by hand.

Pecorino cheese is also made in Sicily near Palermo. Recent improvements in irrigation have allowed Sicilian farmers to increase their crops threefold, enabling the sheep to graze on the lands left fallow.

The farmers make the cheese by hand and age it for an average period of six months. Pecorino cured for only two months is considered fresh, while aged Pecorino is cured for one year.

I find Sicilian Pecorino to have more bite than Sardinian Pecorino Romano, making the tip of your tongue tingle. The Sicilian cheese may also be more oily. Peppercorns are sometimes added to the cheese to give it even greater flavor.

All types of Pecorino store well in the refrigerator and, if wrapped well in foil or plastic wrap, have a shelf life up to one year.

Italian Farmer, Sicily Italy

Nutritional Content Per One-Ounce (28 grams) Serving	
PECORINO ROMANO	
Calories	114
Protein	7.98 g
Carbohydrates	trace
Fat	9.07 g
Calcium	325 mg
Iron	.20 mg
Vitamin A	8 µg*
B₁ (Thiamine)	8 µg*
B₂ (Riboflavin)	132 µg*
Niacin	56 µg*
Sodium	339 mg

*µg = microgram, 1/1000 of a milligram.

Pecorino Toscano (Toscanello)

Pecorino Toscano (Peck ō rē´ no Tōs káh no), frequently called Toscanello, (Tōs kah nél no) is a semi-hard cheese which has a mildly piquant flavor and a pleasant graininess in texture. Made originally in Tuscany, Toscanello is made from sheep's milk and is aged for three to five months.

Toscanello has a smooth texture broken here and there by small holes. Its body ranges in color from pale yellow to gold, with a smooth, hard rind which is brownish in color.

Toscanello is an excellent table cheese and an ideal salad cheese as well. It may also be grated and used in casseroles, potato, pasta and rice dishes.

Store under refrigeration tightly wrapped in aluminum foil or clear plastic wrap. When stored properly, Toscanello will maintain its flavor for four to six months.

Nutritional Content
Per One-Ounce (28 grams) Serving

PECORINO TOSCANO (TOSCANELLO)

Calories	104
Protein	7.4 g
Carbohydrates	trace
Fat	8.3 g
Calcium	300 mg
Iron	182 µg*
Vitamin A	7 µg*
B$_1$ (Thiamine)	8 µg*
B$_2$ (Riboflavin)	120 µg*
Niacin	50 µg*
Sodium	314 mg

*µg = microgram, 1/1000 of a milligram.

Caciotta

There are many varieties of Caciotta (Kah chō´ tah) cheese. The name Caciotta is more a generic term denoting any number of small, mild cheeses. Some Caciotta cheeses are made from cow's milk, while others are made from goat's or sheep's milk or a mixture thereof.

Caciotta are generally small cheeses, weighing two pounds or so. Aged only from two to three weeks, the various Caciotta cheeses are mild to slightly piquant in flavor. While some Caciottas are creamy and semi-soft, others have drier, flakier textures. Their color varies from creamy white to golden yellow.

All varieties of Caciotta are excellent table cheeses which may be served with mild red or white wines, crusty bread, fruits and raw vegetables. The creamier Caciottas make excellent sandwiches combined with seasoned or cured meats while the firmer Caciottas are ideal in green salads and on antipasto platters.

Keep all varieties of Caciotta under refrigeration in tight-fitting aluminum foil or clear plastic wrap. The cheese should maintain its freshness for fifteen to thirty days.

Use a cheese wire to cut the creamy Caciottas to obtain cleanly sliced portions, and a sharp kitchen knife to cut the firmer varieties.

Nutritional Content Per One-Ounce (28 grams) Serving	
CACIOTTA MADE FROM COW'S MILK	
Calories	92
Protein	5.85 g
Carbohydrates	.28 g
Fat	7.56 g
Calcium	172 µg*
Iron	---
Vitamin A	90 µg*
B_1 (Thiamine)	20 µg*
B_2 (Riboflavin)	87 µg*
Niacin	87 µg*
Sodium	271 mg

*µg = microgram, 1/1000 of a milligram.

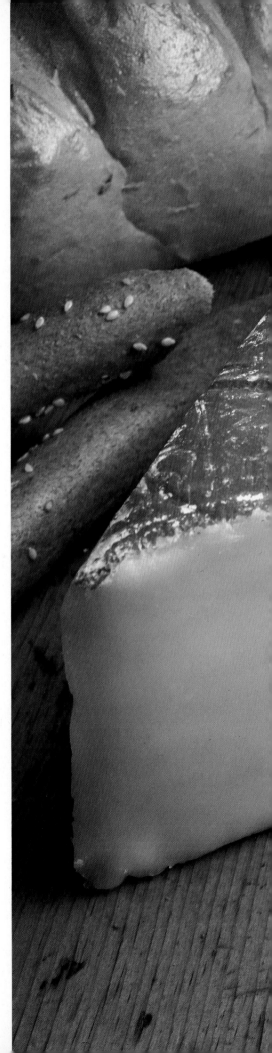

Fontina

Fontina (Fon tē´ nah) is considered to be one of the top ten cheeses in the world because it is a superb table cheese and an excellent cooking cheese as well. Made since the eleventh century, Fontina ripens for two to three months before it develops its characteristic creamy, nutty flavor which is reminiscent of Swiss Emmenthal or Gruyère cheese. This magnificent cheese is ivory to golden yellow in color, firm and smooth in texture. The body of the cheese is broken here and there by tiny holes.

The authentic Fontina cheese is made from the milk of cows who graze in a rigidly defined area in the mountains of northern Italy near the Swiss and French borders — the Aosta Valley. Only the cheese that comes from this valley is allowed by law to bear the name Fontina Val d'Aosta.

Fontal and Fontinella are cheeses very similar to Fontina but are manufactured outside of the Aosta Valley.

Fontina's rich body makes it ideal in recipes because it melts evenly and smoothly. One of the best-known recipes is the Italian Fonduta (fondue) made with fresh Fontina, white truffles and white wine. This exquisite cheese enriches rice, vegetable and pasta dishes.

As a table cheese, serve Fontina with crackers, whole grain breads, fresh fruit or crisp, raw vegetables. A light wine or a not-too-sweet iced tea will bring out the cheese's pleasant flavor.

Fontina is a cheese that appeals to the young and old — to the sophisticated and uninitiated alike.

Store Fontina under constant refrigeration. Always protect the open cut of cheese with tightly wrapped foil or plastic wrap. Fontina stays fresh for at least four months. Its flavor, however, will become more pungent. If not wrapped correctly, the edges will darken and become dry.

Always serve the cheese at room temperature so that its full flavor will be realized.

Nutritional Content Per One-Ounce (28 grams) Serving	
FONTINA	
Calories	90
Protein	6.72 g
Carbohydrates	trace
Fat	7.09 g
Calcium	244 mg
Iron	84 μg*
Vitamin A	118 μg*
B$_1$ (Thiamine)	3 μg*
B$_2$ (Riboflavin)	126 μg*
Niacin	56 μg*
Sodium	182 mg
*μg = microgram, 1/1000 of a milligram.	

Provolone

Most of us do not need an introduction to Provolone (Prō vō lō´ nay) as this is the cheese we have often seen hanging in an Italian delicatessen. Provolone, as Caciocavallo, Ragusano, Mozzarella and Scamorza, belongs to the family of Pasta Filata cheeses which are cheeses whose curds are kneaded and molded into a variety of shapes.

The recipe for making Provolone is an ancient one, for Provolone was a favorite cheese among the ancient Romans. In the first century, Columella, an agricultural writer, told his readers how to make Provolone cheese in a way which closely parallels the modern-day method of making the cheese.

The art of cheesemaking lay dormant in the Dark Ages but flourished once again in the Middle Ages. In the 1500's Caciocavallo was exported in boatloads from Cagliari in Sardinia to Naples, Rome, Livorno (Leghorn), Marseilles and Barcelona.

Provolone is made from whole cow's milk which can either be pasteurized or unpasteurized. Provolone made with unpasteurized milk has a richer, more mellow taste because the milk itself is rich in bacteria. When winter milk is used, the body of the cheese is white in color, whereas when summer milk is used, the cheese is straw yellow in color.

After the milk is heated and the whey is drained from the curd, the curd is then sectioned, shredded and stretched into long, tough fibers which are cut and immersed in hot water and whey. These fibers are then kneaded by hand into a variety of shapes. We are most familiar with the round and pear-shaped cheeses as well as those in the shape of salami ranging in size from two to eighty pounds.

However, Provolone may be made into whatever shape the cheesemaker wishes — piglets, bottles, animal heads. The Emperor Augustus liked to eat his cheese in the shape of horses' heads!

After the Provolone is molded into shape, the cheese is hung by cords of raffia which allow it to cure evenly on all sides. The length of curing determines how mild or sharp the cheese will be. Mild Provolone is aged two to three months while sharp Provolone is aged seven months to two years. Americans, as a rule, prefer milder cheese, and for that reason Provolone exported here from Italy is often milder than that made for the domestic market. Mild Provolone has a smoother texture than the aged cheese which has a more granular body.

Provolone is mildly piquant to piquant in flavor depending upon the length of curing time. It is an excellent table cheese accompanied by a full-bodied wine of your choice. Provolone is often served with luncheon meats such as salami and prosciutto. The mild Provolone goes well with bologna, mortadella or boiled ham. In addition, Provolone is used in many recipes adding both flavor and zest to characteristically Italian dishes.

Provolone stores well under refrigeration for six to eight months if wrapped in tight-fitting plastic wrap or aluminum foil. The flavor of the cheese will improve with age.

Nutritional Content Per One-Ounce (28 grams) Serving	
PROVOLONE	
Calories	97
Protein	7.14 g
Carbohydrates	---
Fat	7.56 g
Calcium	247 mg
Iron	.14 mg
Niacin	.17 mg
Vitamin A	15 μg*
B_1 (Thiamine)	.006 mg
B_2 (Riboflavin)	.23 mg
Sodium	242 mg
*μg = microgram, 1/1000 of a milligram.	

Mozzarella

Italian Mozzarella (Mōtts ah rél lah), often known as "wet" Mozzarella, is very different from its American imitation. Having originated in the sixteenth century, Mozzarella is a snow-white, soft cheese saturated with its own creamy whey. The cheese is made from the milk of the water buffalo or cow's milk or a mixture of both. Being a fresh cheese, it should be eaten as soon as possible. Smoked Mozzarella and Scamorza, a cheese very similar to Mozzarella, are not as perishable and are widely available in a variety of shapes.

Mozzarella is used in many Italian dishes and is well known to Americans as a topping for pizza and as a main ingredient in baked macaroni dishes. I have not included many recipes with Mozzarella because it is so well known to the American public. However, I do suggest that you use the fresh "wet" Mozzarella, which is imported from Italy, in appetizers, salads and on cold cut platters. Serve this delicate, moist Mozzarella cheese as a table cheese seasoned with salt, freshly ground pepper and a dressing of the finest extra virgin olive oil. Accompanied with crusty Italian bread and a light wine, Mozzarella will make an exquisitely delicious, but utterly simple dish.

The smoked or drier Mozzarellas are also good for eating but many prefer them as cooking cheeses.

Nutritional Content Per One-Ounce (28 grams) Serving	
"Wet" MOZZARELLA	
Calories	68
Protein	5.10 g
Carbohydrates	.53 g
Fat	5.04 g
Calcium	113 mg
Iron	56 µg*
Vitamin A	53 µg*
B$_1$ (Thiamine)	14 µg*
B$_2$ (Riboflavin)	142 µg*
Niacin	112 µg*
Sodium	62 mg

*µg = microgram, 1/1000 of a milligram.

Taleggio

Taleggio (Tah lédge ō) is a semi-soft cheese with a pleasant, tangy flavor. Made from cow's milk, the body of the cheese is finely textured and is white to straw yellow in color.

Taleggio ripens in the natural caves of Valsassina in Lombardy. In this humid and cool environment mold spores settle and ripen on the surface of the cheese and within six weeks Taleggio develops its characteristic tangy taste.

An excellent table cheese, Taleggio complements a cheese and cracker tray. Best accompanied by a red wine, Taleggio can hold its own with seasoned meats. The tanginess of the cheese adds zest to fresh garden salads as well as to cold pasta salads.

Taleggio is not as successful as a cooking cheese and should be used primarily as a table cheese and with cold dishes.

As with all cheeses, Taleggio should be served at room temperature and stored under refrigeration. Somewhat more perishable than the other cheeses we have discussed, Taleggio should be kept for no more than one month as it tends to develop a sharp acid taste if stored too long in the refrigerator.

Nutritional Content Per One-Ounce (28 grams) Serving	
TALEGGIO	
Calories	89
Protein	5.43 g
Carbohydrates	.20 g
Fat	7.42 g
Calcium	154 mg
Iron	---
Vitamin A	85 μg*
B$_1$ (Thiamine)	19 μg*
B$_2$ (Riboflavin)	82 μg*
Niacin	82 μg*
Sodium	176 mg

*μg = microgram, 1/1000 of a milligram.

Mascarpone

Mascarpone (mah scar pō´ nay) is a rich, fresh cheese with the texture of a thick whipped cream. Heaven in each and every mouthful, Mascarpone may be easily blended with shredded or powdered chocolate, fruits or liqueurs to make mouth-watering desserts.

While Mascarpone is primarily a dessert cheese, it can also be used as a creamy base in pasta sauces.

Mascarpone forms the basis of Torte de Formaggio — layered cheese cakes — which consist of layers of cheese and of other foods such as salmon, peppers and fruits. Mascarpone combines beautifully with other cheeses — Gorgonzola, Grana Padano, Pecorino Romano, Taleggio, Italico — to make many varieties of layered cheeses.

The very popular Torta Basilico is made from Mascarpone, Grana Padano, Pecorino Romano, basil, pine nuts and olive oil.

Torta Gorgonzola/Mascarpone (Tór tah Gōr gōn zō´ lah Mah scar pō´ nay) joins the creamy sweetness of Mascarpone with the tang and bite of Gorgonzola. Spread on crackers or served with sweet dark grapes, Torta Gorgonzola/Mascarpone is delightful. Spread this cheese on celery sticks and you have a very tasty appetizer.

Available in specialty food shops, these cheeses make excitingly different hors d'oeuvres.

Torte de Formaggio are very perishable and usually have a shelf life of about two weeks to one month. Although it is possible to preserve them longer, the cheese will begin to suffer after a period of thirty days.

The usual shelf life for Mascarpone is two weeks, so be sure that the product is fresh when you buy it. Some brands of Mascarpone may last upwards to three months under refrigeration if the package remains sealed. Once opened, however, the cheese should be eaten within two weeks.

Nutritional Content Per One-Ounce (28 grams) Serving	
MASCARPONE	
Calories	128
Protein	1.46 g
Carbohydrates	1.15 g
Fat	13.10 g
Calcium	19 mg
Iron	.056 g
Vitamin A	120 μg*
B_1 (Thiamine)	3 μg*
B_2 (Riboflavin)	62 μg*
Niacin	28 μg*
Sodium	17 mg
*μg = microgram, 1/1000 of a milligram.	

Nutritional Content Per One-Ounce (28 grams) Serving	
TORTA GORGONZOLA/MASCARPONE	
Calories	111
Protein	3.30 g
Carbohydrates	.64 g
Fat	10.64 g
Calcium	57 mg
Iron	.07 g
Vitamin A	119 μg*
B_1 (Thiamine)	3 μg*
B_2 (Riboflavin)	56 μg*
Niacin	140 μg*
Sodium	99 mg
*μg = microgram, 1/1000 of a milligram.	

GLOSSARY OF TERMS AND INGREDIENTS

Cheese

(Only those terms not described in detail in the introduction of the book are defined below.)

1. Cultures
Micro-organisms added to the milk in order to give a cheese its specific character.

2. Rennet
An animal or vegetable enzyme-releasing agent used to curdle the milk

3. Ricotta
A cheese made from cow's or sheep's milk. When fresh, it is a soft cheese, similar to creamy cottage cheese but with a more cohesive texture and a mellow, less acid taste. Used in desserts, casseroles and in sauces, ricotta is an excellent cooking cheese because its mildness blends well with other flavors and its creamy texture tends to bind the ingredients together.

4. Ricotta salata
A harder variety of ricotta, aged for fifteen to twenty days. Snowy white in color and compact in texture, this type of ricotta is used as a table cheese and in salads as well.

When ricotta is aged for eight months, it is used primarily as a grating cheese. Ricotta is a tasty cheese with a pleasantly pronounced flavor.

5. Table cheese
A cheese that is served either by itself, with bread or crackers or with fruit, raw vegetables or cured meats. Many cheeses, whether mild or strong in flavor, fall into this category.

6. Whey
The liquid part of the milk which is drained off when the curd is formed.

7. Curd
The coagulated part of the milk used to make cheese.

Herbs and Spices

1. Marjoram
A moderately pungent herb of the mint family which has both a sweet and spicy flavor with a suggestion of cloves or mint. Marjoram is used in tomato dishes, fish, veal, lamb and sausage dishes and often as a substitute for oregano.

2. Rosemary
A spicy, pungent-flavored herb which traditionally has been considered the herb of friendship and remembrance. Used in pork, lamb and chicken roasts, rosemary is a popular herb in Italy growing wild throughout the country.

3. Oregano
A strong-flavored herb almost always used dried. It is a popular herb used extensively in Italian cooking.

4. Basil
A versatile, flavorful herb of the mint family used fresh or dried in sauces, dressings, with vegetables, meats, poultry and fish.

5. Sage
A pungent herb used in sauces, gravies and stuffing. Sage is best when used fresh.

6. Nutmeg
A bittersweet spice which is the dried seed of the fruit of an evergreen tree. Nutmeg blends well with many foods and is used in many types of dishes adding aromatic flavor and richness. Fresh nutmeg is considered far superior to that already ground and special nutmeg graters are available for this purpose.

7. Parsley
A flat-leaved herb of delicate flavor used in meat, poultry and fish dishes, and in sauces and vegetables as well.

Pasta and Bread Shop, Rome Italy

Fruits and Nuts

1. Pignoli (pine nuts)
Small oblong-shaped seeds of a pine tree which are sweet and nutty in flavor with a chewy consistency. Pignoli are used in baking, sauces and salads. Usually available in baking section of supermarkets or in Italian delicatessens, pignoli are usually shelled and packaged in glass bottles.

2. Golden raisins
More delicate in taste than the darker variety of raisins.

Flours and Grains

3. Buckwheat groats (kasha)
Coarsely ground grain native to Asia. Buckwheat can be finely ground into a flour which is used for pancakes or coarsely ground and called groats or kasha. Kasha can be served as a variation of polenta either by itself or mixed with cornmeal.

4. Polenta
A cornmeal dish of northern Italy which can be served either hot or cold. (See page 139 for detailed description.) It is served with a variety of sauces and is used both as a first and second course of the meal.

5. Semolina flour
Milled from hard durum wheat, semolina is a pale yellow, coarse flour unlike all-purpose flour that has a powdery texture. Used in making dried pasta, semolina makes a very elastic dough which can be rolled out to paper thinness. Pasta made from this flour has a better texture and holds its shape longer than pasta made from other types of flour. Because it is so coarse, however, it is difficult to knead and is often mixed with other flours. It is not used in egg pasta or in any light pasta.

Pasta and Rice

6. Arborio rice
Short-grained Italian rice used in making risotto. It has the unique characteristic of releasing a creamy liquid when cooked. (See page 124 for a more detailed description.)

7. Fresh pasta
Under the heading of fresh pasta are those types of pasta which are made with softer flour than dried pasta, i.e., macaroni. In some regions of Italy fresh pasta is made with eggs.

8. Cannelloni
Large rectangles of noodle dough rolled into a tubular shape, usually stuffed with meat and white sauce and baked in the oven.

9. Tagliatelle
Long flat egg noodles which originated in Bologna. Tagliatelle are considered such an important contribution to Bolognese culinary art that a solid gold tagliatelle noodle with its ideal measurements of 1 mm thick and 6 mm wide is encased in sealed glass in Bologna's Chamber of Commerce!

10. Tortellini
Small ring-shaped pasta, native to Bologna, filled with a variety of stuffings, usually meat or cheese.

11. Dried pasta (macaroni)
Macaroni or dried pasta is made from a harder flour than fresh pasta. The best Italian dried pasta is made from durum wheat flour which has more gluten than ordinary flour. Gluten in wheat gives dough its elasticity and tension allowing it to maintain its shape and integrity in cooking and not get overly soft or fall apart.

12. Manicotti
Large tube-shaped macaroni usually stuffed with ricotta and mozzarella, topped with tomato sauce and then baked.

13. Mostaccioli
Short tubed-shaped macaroni about 1½ inches in length cut diagonally. Also called *penne*.

14. Rigatoni
Large tubular macaroni with ridged surface smaller than manicotti. Rigatoni is excellent with meat sauces and cheese because it scoops up the sauce within its hollow center.

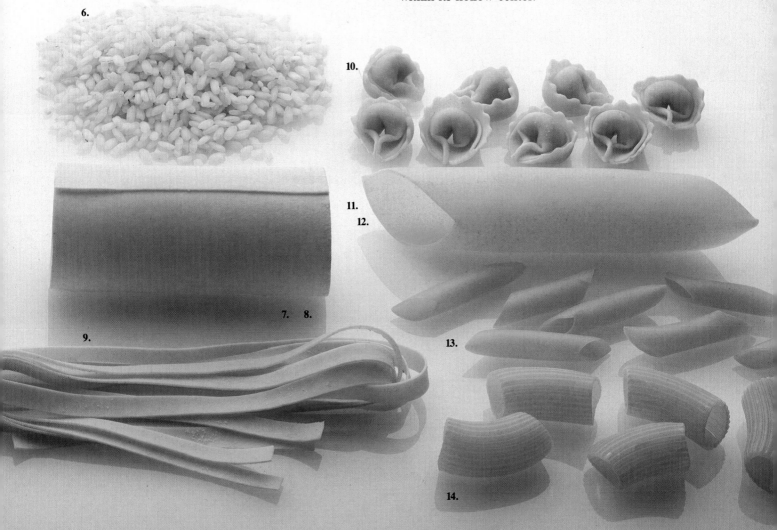

Vegetables

1. Zucchini
Green summer squash, cylindrical in shape. The smaller zucchini are best for eating while the larger plants are used for stuffing. A versatile vegetable because of its mild taste, zucchini can be boiled, fried or baked and are used in casseroles, pasta, rice, meat and vegetable dishes.

2. Truffles
A tuberous plant prized for its exceptional flavor and esteemed as a delicacy since Classical times. Truffles grow spontaneously underground and may grow as deep as a foot under the surface. Because of this, man must use the aid of dogs and hogs to harvest them. There are both black and white truffles, the white said to be more delicate in flavor.

3. Yellow peppers
Bell-shaped peppers that are yellow-orange in color. These peppers are very sweet and are exquisite roasted.

4. Savoy cabbage
Crinkly leaved, deep green in color, Savoy cabbage is not as compact as white cabbage. It has a pleasant taste and is used both in salads and in cooked dishes.

Vegetables

Boston lettuce
Round in shape, smaller than iceberg lettuce, with small silken leaves. Similar to Bibb lettuce, Boston lettuce has a delicate flavor.

Chicory
Slightly bitter in taste, chicory is known also as curly endive. Chicory grows in a head, and has curly, ragged edged leaves with dark green outer leaves and yellowish green center leaves. The outer leaves are stronger in flavor than the center leaves.

Fennel
Somewhat similar to celery in appearance, fennel has a mild licorice flavor. When raw it is used in salads and antipasto platters. It is also braised or baked and served as a vegetable in its own right. Its leaves are often used to flavor sauces while its seeds are used to flavor sausage.

Italian peppers
These peppers are not really Italian as all peppers originated in South and Central America, but they are so called because Italian Americans, especially on the East Coast of the United States, use them often in their cooking. These peppers have a tapered shape and are light green in color. They are less fleshy and milder in taste than dark green bell peppers. Used in a variety of dishes, they are either roasted or fried.

Endive (French or Belgian)
A member of the chicory family, endive has a
tapered shape with tightly packed white leaves edged
in light green or yellow. Slightly bitter in taste,
endive is eaten raw in salads and served as a cooked
vegetable as well.

Escarole
Also a member of the chicory family like endive,
escarole has larger, smoother leaves and is generally
larger in size than its cousin.

Leek
A vegetable that belongs, like onion and garlic, to
the lily family. Leeks look like large scallions (green
onions) and have a large white bulb and long, fleshy
green leaves. Having a mild onion taste, leeks are
used in soups and sauces and are often served as a
side dish with a mild cheese sauce.

Romaine lettuce
Also called Cos lettuce, Romaine lettuce is long and
tapered in shape with dark green textured outer
leaves and greenish yellow inner leaves. This type of
lettuce is more chewy and pronounced in flavor than
iceberg lettuce.

Meats

1. Pepperoni
Dried Italian-American sausage of spicy, hot flavor used on pizza, in sandwiches and in antipasto platters as well. As such, this type of sausage does not exist in Italy.

2. Pancetta
Italian cured bacon. Made from the stomach (pancia) of the hog, pancetta is made of thin layers of meat which are lightly spiced and salted and rolled into a salami shape. It is dry-cured and has a delicate taste and fragrance. Pancetta is used in sauces, soups and in stuffings and is excellent in sandwiches as well.

3. Milano salami
A finely-ground salami with a mild flavor used in cold cut platters and in antipasti.

4. Prosciutto
Italian dry-cured ham. A specialty of Parma in northern Italy, prosciutto is prepared from the hind legs of specially chosen hogs and is cured for a period of at least twenty-four months. Its exquisitely delicate flavor makes it a favorite with fresh fruit, cold platters, in sandwiches and in cooking as well.

5. Mortadella
Italian bologna. Mortadella is a cooked Italian specialty sausage made from cuts of choice pork. Having originated in Bologna in the fourteenth century, mortadella derives its name from the mortars (mortai) in which the meat was originally pounded. Mortadella is used most often as a luncheon meat and in antipasto platters.

Wine

Madeira

A wine made on the Portuguese island of Madeira in the North Atlantic, north of the Canary Islands. Madeira is used to flavor sauces and desserts. Depending upon the type of Madeira, the wine can be dry, sweet or full-bodied.

Madeira Vineyard

Marsala

A Sicilian wine which can either be sweet or dry. It may be served as an aperitif or used in desserts or cheese dishes.

Marsala Grape Harvest

Pastry and Cookies

Amaretto cookies
Small Italian hard cookies made from egg whites, sugar and flavoring.

Puff pastry
A light, flaky, buttery pastry which can be used in hors d'oeuvres or in desserts. Available fresh or frozen.

Sauces and Dressings

1. Extra virgin olive oil
The finest grade of olive oil made from cold pressing select Italian olives without adding heat or chemicals. Extra virgin olive oil has less than 1% acidity which accounts for its rich, mellow flavor with no bitter aftertaste. Used as a dressing for salads and vegetables, it is also used in cooking because of its stability at high temperatures and for its excellent flavor.

2. Stock
Liquid made from the bones and flesh of meat, fish or poultry along with vegetables and herbs. Stock forms the basis of many sauces and soups adding flavor, body and nutrition.

3. Béchamel sauce
A white sauce made from flour, butter and milk used with vegetables, in pasta dishes and as a basis for other sauces.

4. Mornay sauce
A variation of Béchamel or white sauce. Cheese, and sometimes eggs, are added to the basic sauce.

Introduction

Santa Maria del Fiore, Florence, Italy

Italian cheeses range in flavor from mild to pungent. While each individual cheese will be discussed in detail in the following chapter, a basic rule of thumb in serving cheese is to complement the flavor of the cheese with the food with which it is served. You will not want to serve robust cheeses with a mild sauce because the cheese will overpower the sauce. The beverage you choose should be selected on the same basis: mild wines with delicate flavors and more robust wines with stronger-flavored cheeses. A mellow cheese like Parmigiano-Reggiano should be served with mild-flavored meats, vegetables such as artichokes and asparagus and mild red or white wines. A robust cheese like Pecorino Romano should be served with seasoned meats, oil-cured black olives or green olives and full-bodied red wines.

Evening Entertainment

Have on hand dry white and dry red wines to serve with the following cheese hors d'oeuvres. Red wine will complement the stronger cheeses — Gorgonzola, Torta Gorgonzola/Mascarpone, mature Fontina and aged Provolone while dry white wines will go well with Bel Paese® , mild Provolone, Fontina and Mozzarella.

1. Piedmont Fondue (with Fontina) (page 67)
Carrot and Zucchini Sticks, Broccoli Flowerets,
  Cauliflowerets, Whole Tomatoes, Bread Sticks
A Gorgonzola Pyramid (page 70)

2. Bel Paese® Meringue Quiche (page 69)
Torta Gorgonzola/Mascarpone with Raw Vegetables
  (page 67)

3. Gorgonzola Deviled Eggs (page 71)
Mixed Green Salad
Provolone Teasers (page 73)
Gorgonzola "Sea Urchin" (page 71)
Frankfurter Hors d'oeuvres (page 75)

Puff Pastry
Since puff pastry should be piping hot when served, it might be best to seat your guests first.

4. Serve a combination of two of the following:
Provolone Puff Pastry (page 72)
Bel Paese® Puff Pastry (page 73)
Zucchini/Fontina Puff Pastry (page 72)

5. La Bel Quiche (page 69)
Torta Gorgonzola/Mascarpone Nut Canape (page 71)
Carrot and Celery Sticks
Broccoli Flowerets and Cauliflowerets

6. Gorgonzola "Sea Urchin" (page 71)
Pastry Shells with Bel Paese® and Mushrooms
  (page 74)

7. Mozzarella/Fontina Rice Quiche (page 127)
Celery, Fennel, Assorted Olives

Afternoon Entertaining

1. Bel Paese® Fondue Croquettes
  (page 66)
Green Salad with Extra Virgin
  Olive Oil/Red Wine Vinegar
  Dressing
Angelo's Delight (page 155)
Espresso or Coffee

2. Seared Provolone Slices with
  Herb Dressing (page 87)
Italian Bread
Bottled Marinated Olive Salad
Fresh Fruit

3. Bel Paese® Cutlets (page 86)
Raw Vegetable Salad with Creamy
  Italian Dressing

4. Golden Brown Provolone
  Sandwiches with Tomato Sauce
  (page 87)
Fresh Garden Salad with Raw
  Vegetables

5. Chicken Salad with Provolone
  (page 82)
Zucchini with
  Parmigiano-Reggiano (page 104)
Croissants or Hard Rolls
Lemon Meringue Pie

6. Medallion Soup with Cream of
  Celery Soup (page 78)
Rice Salad with Toscanello
  (page 82)
Bel Paese® Medallions
Bread Sticks, Sesame Seed
  Crackers, Buttery-type Crackers
Fresh Fruit with Mascarpone
  Topping
Coffee/Tea

7. Asparagus Pie (page 101)
Salad
Amaretto Cookies and
  Mascarpone (page 155)

8. Eggplant with Bel Paese® and
  Prosciutto (page 105)
Fresh Rolls
Fruit Salad

9. Grilled Polenta with
  Parmigiano-Reggiano (page 142)
Caesar Salad
Crusty Italian Bread

*Bel Paese® Fondue Croquettes, Salad,
Angelo's Delight, and Espresso*

Baked Fillet of Sole, Salad, Parmigiano-Reggiano Potatoes and Pound Cake with Mascarpone Topping

Unexpected Company

For unexpected company, a first course of risotto, pasta, soup or a side dish of potatoes will stretch your planned meal. The recipes, in addition, are so unique that they will elicit praise and beams of satisfaction.

1. Baked Fillet of Sole
Fresh Garden Salad with Oil and Vinegar Dressing
Parmigiano-Reggiano Potatoes (page 131)
Pound Cake with Mascarpone Topping

2. Medallion Soup with Cream of Potato Soup
  (page 78)
Broiled Lamb Chops
Roasted Bell Pepper Salad with Extra Virgin Olive
  Oil and Oregano
Dinner Rolls
Chocolate Pudding with Whipped Cream Topping

3. Cabbage/Onion Soup with Provolone (page 79)
Sirloin Steak
French Style Green Beans Sautéed with Garlic and
  Extra Virgin Olive Oil
Chocolate Layer Cake

4. Baked Chicken Parmigiano (page 150)
Brussels Sprouts
Spinach
Baked Potatoes with Butter
Apple Pie

5. Veal Cutlets with Bel Paese® Medallion (page 145)
Steamed Artichokes
Peas and Onions
Mashed Potatoes
Mascarpone "Parfait" (page 156)

6. Breaded Chicken Cutlets
Ripe Tomato Salad with Basil Leaves and Olive Oil
Potato Surprise (page 132)
Ice Cream Cake

7. Potato Balls in Broth (page 77) or
  Parmigiano Gnocchi (page 135)
Broiled Pork Chops
Red Cabbage Salad (page 82)
Italian Cookies/Coffee

Special Occasions/Leisurely Family Meals

The following recipes are ideal for special occasions and for leisurely family meals when you have enough time at your disposal.

1. Tortellini with Bel Paese®
  (page 117)
Roast Chicken
Garden Salad with Oil and
  Vinegar
Amaretto Cookies with
  Mascarpone (page 155)

2. Spinach Pasta with Gorgonzola
  Sauce (page 119)
Roast Beef
Peas and Carrots
Cheesecake

3. Bel Paese® Pastry Gnocchi
  (page 135)
Breaded Veal Cutlets
Asparagus
Mascarpone Graham Cracker Pie
  (page 153)

4. Tagliatelle with Cream Sauce
  (page 115)
Roast Turkey or Capon
Green Beans with Almonds
Fresh Fruit

5. Prosciutto/Mozzarella Appetizer
  (page 69)
Lasagna with White and Red
  Sauces (page 121)
Broccoli Spears with Butter
  and Lemon
Fruit Gelatin with
  Mascarpone Topping

6. Risotto Milanese (page 125)
Roast Pork
Asparagus with Béchamel Sauce
  (page 101)
Tiramisù (page 153)

7. Semolina Polenta with Pecorino
  and Salt Pork (page 142)
Grilled Fillet of Red Snapper or
  Cod with Lemon, Oil and
  Parsley Sauce
Salad
Sherbet

Tortellini with Bel Paese®,
Roast Chicken, Salad and
Amaretto Cookies with Mascarpone

59

Casual Get-Togethers/Easy Entertaining

For casual get-togethers emphasize one dish and then complement it with soup, salad or vegetable dish. This type of menu planning goes equally well for everyday meals as well.

Pasta and Salad

1. Rigatoni with Beef Stew (page 146)
Roasted Pepper Salad

2. Meatballs Romano with Spaghetti (page 147)
Garden Salad with Raw Vegetables

3. Macaroni with Cauliflower, Raisins, Pine Nuts
and Pecorino Romano (page 123)
Mixed Green Salad

Homemade Pizza

1. Cream of Spinach Soup
Ham and Gorgonzola Pizza (page 98)

2. Bel Paese®/Prosciutto Calzone (page 95)
Garden Salad

3. Split Pea Soup
Provolone Pizza (page 98)

Bel Paese®/Prosciutto Calzone and Garden Salad

Northern Italy

Entertaining Outdoors

1. Southern Fried Chicken
Bel Paese® and Macaroni Salad (page 81)
Bel Paese® Medallions
Crusty Italian Bread

2. Marinated Artichoke Salad with Prosciutto and
  Grana Padano (page 82)
Mushroom Salad with Bel Paese® (page 80)
Breaded Veal Cutlets
Fresh Rolls

3. Zucchini Omelette (wrap omelette in foil
  to keep warm)
Breaded Chicken Cutlets
Bel Paese® and Taleggio Wedges
Fresh Bread

4. Special Bel Paese® Salad (page 80)
Rice Salad with Toscanello (page 82)
Black Olives
Carrot and Celery Sticks
Bakery Rolls

5. Deviled Eggs
Chicken Salad
Raw Spinach Salad
Parmigiano-Reggiano Cheese Bread (page 97)

6. Tuna Salad
Bel Paese® and Macaroni Salad (page 81)
Ripe Tomato Slices
Parmigiano Buttermilk Biscuits (page 97)

7. Meatballs
Fried Eggplant
Parmigiano and Toscanello Wedges
Italian Bread

8. Assorted Raw Vegetables (broccoli, carrots,
  cauliflower, radishes and zucchini)
Assorted Cheeses (Bel Paese®, Gorgonzola,
  Parmigiano-Reggiano, Taleggio, Toscanello)
Fresh Fruit
Pumpernickel or Crusty Italian Bread

Assorted Raw Vegetables, Assorted Cheeses, Fresh Fruit and Pumpernickel or Crusty Italian Bread

Cheese and Other Foods — A New Dimension

Cheese can enliven a standard menu by offering new alternatives to familiar dishes. Taleggio, Provolone or Caciotta can add zest and tanginess to the most familiar salads. Bel Paese®, Fontina and Gorgonzola can be combined with cream to make luscious sauces for pasta, potatoes, rice and vegetable dishes. Parmigiano, Grana Padano and Provolone can be combined with eggs to make delicious omelettes.

The recipes in this book combine cheese with a great many foods. They are meant to serve as an introduction to cooking with Italian cheese. You will soon be able to develop your own variations.

The ingredients used in our recipes are relatively easy to buy; most of them are already on your pantry shelf. We have sometimes included two versions of a recipe — a "time-consuming" version for those times when you have the desire to make everything "from scratch" and a "quickie" version for those times when you prefer to use a ready-made product. We know that today's homemakers have busy schedules and often do not have the time or inclination to make cooking an all-consuming task. However, we also know that homemade pasta, pie shells, pizza and gnocchi taste better than do store-bought products. It is fortunate that we can now buy fresh pasta in the specialty section of our supermarkets and at other retail shops. We can really enjoy the best of both worlds!

We have left out salt in many of the recipes because the cheeses already contain some salt. You may add salt if you wish.

These recipes can be adapted to other Italian cheeses which we may not have mentioned. You need only to think about the characteristics of any cheese and ask yourself:

1. It is mild or strong?
2. Will it melt easily?
3. Will it overpower other ingredients in a recipe?
4. Will it overpower other foods with which it is served?
5. Will it be complemented better by a white or a red sauce?

Use these recipes as a starting point and substitute similar cheeses to see how they complement or contrast with one another. Some disasters may result, but some masterpieces may also. This book is meant to stimulate you to create your own recipes after getting a little bit of practice and familiarity with Italian cheeses.

This book is not intended as "The Last Word" but as an introduction, a first course, if you will, in Italian cheese cookery.

Prosciutto/Fresh Mozzarella Appetizer, Baked Chicken Parmigiano, Asparagus Pie, Cauliflower/Provolone Puff Pastry, Special Bel Paese® Salad, Pasta with Mascarpone/Prociutto Sauce.

Bel Paese® Fondue

Bel Paese® Fondue

This recipe is excellent when served over polenta, page 139, or crusty Italian bread, or with crisp bread sticks. Allow about an hour to make the polenta. If you do not have time to make it from scratch, use instant polenta available in the specialty section of your grocery store and in Italian delicatessens.

1 lb. Bel Paese® cheese*, cut into thin slices
1 cup milk
  Cold water
¼ cup butter
4 to 6 egg yolks, beaten
  Truffle (optional)

*Remove wax coating and moist, white crust from cheese.

Place cheese in shallow bowl. Add milk and just enough water to cover cheese. Let stand for 30 minutes.

In medium saucepan melt butter. Add cheese and about ⅓ cup diluted milk, reserving the remaining diluted milk. Cook over low heat until cheese melts, stirring constantly. Add more diluted milk if mixture is too thick. Remove from heat. Add egg yolks. Mix vigorously. Transfer mixture to double boiler. Cook over medium heat, stirring constantly with whisk, until fondue is thick and creamy. Water in double boiler should not boil.

Use vegetable brush to clean a white truffle. Peel or shell a black truffle with sharp knife. Slice or cut into small pieces and use as garnish. Serve fondue over polenta pieces.

Serves 6 to 8.

Bel Paese® Fondue Croquettes

7 oz. Bel Paese® cheese*, cut into small pieces
2 tablespoons Béchamel Sauce (below)
1 egg yolk, slightly beaten
1 egg, beaten
½ cup fine dry bread crumbs
  Vegetable oil for frying

*Remove wax coating and moist, white crust from cheese.

In small non-stick saucepan, combine cheese and 2 tablespoons Béchamel Sauce. Cook over low heat until cheese melts, stirring constantly. Remove from heat. Add egg yolk and mix well. Spread into 9-inch square baking dish. Refrigerate until mixture sets, about 20 to 30 minutes.

Cut cheese mixture into 18 pieces about 4 × ¾ inch. Roll with fingers if pieces are soft. Dip each piece in egg and roll in bread crumbs. In medium skillet, heat ⅛ inch oil over medium heat. Fry a few pieces at a time until golden brown, about 30 to 40 seconds, turning once. Drain on paper towels. Serve hot with a fresh garden salad.

Serves 4.

Béchamel Sauce

2 tablespoons butter
2 tablespoons all-purpose flour
¾ cup milk
  White pepper

In small saucepan, melt butter. Stir in flour. Blend in milk. Add white pepper to taste. Cook over medium-low heat, stirring constantly, until thick and bubbly.

Makes ¾ cup.

66

Torta Gorgonzola/Mascarpone with Raw Vegetables

8 oz. Torta Gorgonzola/
  Mascarpone
  Paprika
  Broccoli flowerets
  Carrot sticks
  Cauliflowerets
  Celery sticks
  Radishes

Allow Torta Gorgonzola/
Mascarpone to soften at room
temperature for 15 minutes. In
medium bowl, mash cheese with
wooden spoon to form a paste.
Add dash or two of paprika. Mix
well. Refrigerate for 10 minutes.

Place cheese mixture in center of
large platter. Arrange raw vegetables for dipping around cheese.

Serves 6 to 8.

*Torta Gorgonzola/Mascarpone
with Raw Vegetables*

Piedmont Fondue

8 oz. Fontina, cut into thin slices
  Milk
2 tablespoons heavy cream
2 egg yolks, slightly beaten
8 slices toast

Place cheese in shallow bowl. Add
just enough milk to cover cheese.
Let stand for 1 to 2 hours.

Drain cheese, reserving milk. In
medium saucepan, combine
cheese and cream. Cook over low
heat, until smooth, stirring constantly. Blend in small amount of
reserved milk if fondue is too
thick. Remove from heat. Blend
in egg yolks. Cook over low heat,
until mixture is smooth, stirring
constantly. Serve over toast.

Serves 4 to 6.

Bel Paese® cheese or a creamy
Caciotta can be substituted
for Fontina.

Fonduta Bel Paese®

Fonduta Bel Paese® pictured on page 64

1 clove garlic, cut in half
1½ cups white wine
2 to 4 tablespoons kirsch
3 cups shredded Bel Paese®
  cheese* (about 12 oz.)
3 tablespoons all-purpose flour
  or arrowroot
⅛ teaspoon white pepper
⅛ teaspoon cayenne
  Italian bread

*Remove wax coating and moist,
 white crust from cheese.

Rub fondue dish with garlic clove.
Discard garlic. Heat wine and
kirsch in fondue dish or in double
boiler until just steaming. In
plastic bag shake cheese, flour,
white pepper and cayenne. Add
cheese and flour mixture to wine
and kirsch, stirring constantly with
whisk, until cheese melts and
mixture is smooth. Cut bread into
small slices or chunks for twirling
in fondue.

Serves 12 as hors d'oeuvres or 4
for brunch.

Prosciutto/Fresh Mozzarella Appetizer

½ lb. Prosciutto, thinly sliced
8 oz. fresh "wet" Mozzarella, cut into ½-inch strips
Lettuce leaves (optional)
Extra virgin olive oil
Dried oregano leaves
Freshly ground pepper

Place one or two strips Mozzarella at one end of each slice Prosciutto. Fold Prosciutto over Mozzarella and roll up. Arrange on lettuce-lined serving plate. Drizzle with olive oil. Sprinkle with oregano and pepper.

Serves 6.

Mortadella can be substituted for Prosciutto.

La Bel Quiche

1 9-inch pie crust, unbaked
¼ lb. Prosciutto,
   or fully-cooked ham or
   cooked bacon, crumbled
4 eggs
2 egg yolks
1 cup half-and-half
¼ cup shredded Bel Paese® cheese* (1 oz.)
¼ teaspoon pepper

*Remove wax coating and moist, white crust from cheese.

Preheat oven to 350°F. Pierce bottom of pie crust with fork several times. Bake for 5 minutes. Cool.

Chop Prosciutto. Sprinkle in bottom of pie crust. In medium mixing bowl, combine remaining ingredients. Beat with whisk until fluffy. Pour into cooled pie crust. Bake at 350°F until set, about 35 to 45 minutes. Serve with full-bodied red wine.

Serves 4 to 6.

Bel Paese® Meringue Quiche

Crust

2 cups all-purpose flour
⅛ teaspoon salt
4 egg yolks (reserve 2 egg whites for filling)
1 to 3 tablespoons water
10 tablespoons cold butter, cut into small pieces

Filling

5 oz. Bel Paese® cheese*, cubed
¼ cup half-and-half
½ cup freshly grated Parmigiano-Reggiano (1 oz.)
2 teaspoons minced fresh parsley
⅛ teaspoon salt
⅛ teaspoon ground nutmeg
Dash pepper
2 reserved egg whites

*Remove wax coating and moist, white crust from cheese.

For Crust, combine flour and salt on a board. Make a well in center. Blend egg yolks, and water. Add egg mixture and butter to well. Mix together with fingers until dough is smooth, adding more water if necessary. Shape into a ball. Cover and refrigerate about 30 minutes.

Preheat oven to 350°F. Grease a 9-inch pie plate. Roll out dough on floured board to fit pie plate. Ease dough into pie plate. Trim and flute edge. Pierce bottom of crust with fork several times. Bake for 15 minutes. Cool.

For Filling, in medium mixing bowl, mix Bel Paese®, half-and-half, Parmigiano-Reggiano, parsley, salt, nutmeg and pepper. Set aside.

Place egg whites in small mixing bowl. Beat at high speed of electric mixer until stiff peaks form. Fold into cheese mixture. Pour into cooled crust. Bake at 350°F until set and golden brown, 15 to 20 minutes.

Serves 4.

La Bel Quiche

Torta Gorgonzola/Mascarpone Cocktail Sandwiches

 6 to 8 slices whole wheat or rye bread
½ cup butter or margarine
10 oz. Torta Gorgonzola/Mascarpone
¾ teaspoon Worcestershire sauce
⅛ teaspoon paprika
 2 eggs, beaten
  Vegetable oil for frying

Cut bread into 1½-inch rounds using a biscuit cutter or sharp knife. In large skillet, melt butter over medium heat. Fry bread rounds lightly, turning once. Drain on paper towels.

Allow Torta Gorgonzola/Mascarpone to soften at room temperature for 15 minutes. Press cheese through sieve or food mill or mash until smooth. In small mixing bowl, combine cheese, Worcestershire sauce and paprika. Spread mixture on half the fried bread rounds. Top with remaining rounds to make sandwiches.

Dip each sandwich in egg. In large skillet, heat ⅛ inch oil over medium heat. Fry sandwiches until golden brown, turning once.

Serves 4.

5 oz. Gorgonzola and 5 oz. Mascarpone can be substituted for Torta Gorgonzola/Mascarpone. Press only the Gorgonzola through sieve or food mill, then mix well with Mascarpone.

OPTION: Omit dipping sandwich in egg and omit final frying.

A Gorgonzola Pyramid

 7 oz. Gorgonzola
  Dash paprika
  Dash ground nutmeg
¼ cup fresh bread crumbs
  Lettuce leaves (optional)
  Radishes (optional)
  Rye or whole wheat cocktail bread slices
  (optional)

Allow Gorgonzola to soften at room temperature for 30 minutes. Press cheese through sieve or food mill or mash until smooth. In small mixing bowl, combine cheese, paprika and nutmeg. Refrigerate for about 15 minutes.

Shape cheese mixture into ¾- to 1-inch balls. Roll in bread crumbs. On lettuce-lined serving plate, stack balls into pyramid shape. Serve with radishes and bread slices.

Serves 4 to 6.

Torta Gorgonzola/Mascarpone Cocktail Sandwiches

Gorgonzola "Sea Urchin" with Cognac

8 oz. Gorgonzola
8 oz. fresh ricotta cheese
5 teaspoons cognac or brandy
   Cocktail pretzel sticks

Allow Gorgonzola to soften at room temperature for 30 minutes. In medium mixing bowl, stir Gorgonzola with wooden spoon until smooth and creamy. Stir in ricotta and cognac to form a paste.

Place mixture on serving plate. Shape into ball using back of spoon. Refrigerate until set, at least 1 hour.

Just before serving, pierce ball with pretzel sticks to give it the appearance of a sea urchin. Serve with remaining pretzel sticks.

Serves 8.

Fresh ricotta is similar to a creamy, small curd cottage cheese and is available in the dairy case of your supermarket.

Torta Gorgonzola/Mascarpone Nut Canapé

 8 oz. Torta Gorgonzola/Mascarpone
4½ oz. ground pecans or walnuts
   Rye or other whole grain cocktail bread slices

Allow Torta Gorgonzola/Mascarpone to soften at room temperature for 15 minutes. In medium mixing bowl, blend cheese and nuts to form a paste. Spread on bread slices.

Serves 4.

Gorgonzola Deviled Eggs

3½ oz. Gorgonzola
 4 hard-cooked eggs, peeled
 ½ teaspoon butter, softened
12 black olives, pitted and minced
   Dash Worcestershire sauce
   Lettuce leaves (optional)
   Fresh parsley sprigs (optional)
   Black olives, pitted and sliced (optional)

Allow Gorgonzola to soften at room temperature for 30 minutes. Meanwhile, carefully cut eggs in half lengthwise and remove yolks. Set egg halves aside.

In small mixing bowl, blend cheese and butter until smooth. Add egg yolks and mix well. Stir in olives and Worcestershire sauce.

Spoon mixture into egg halves. Arrange on lettuce-lined plate. Garnish with parsley and olives.

Serves 4.

Gorgonzola "Sea Urchin" with Cognac

Provolone Pastry Cheesesticks

Provolone Pastry Cheesesticks

½ cup + 2 tablespoons all-purpose flour
¼ teaspoon pepper
¼ teaspoon dry mustard
3½ tablespoons cold butter, cut into small pieces
2 egg yolks, slightly beaten
3 tablespoons cold water
3½ oz. mild Provolone*, shredded (about 1 cup)
2 to 3 teaspoons milk
Assorted raw vegetables (optional)

*Remove wax coating from cheese.

Preheat oven to 375°. Grease baking sheet. Set aside.

Combine flour, pepper and mustard on a board. Make a well in center. Add butter pieces to well. Mix with fingertips. In small bowl, blend egg yolks and 1 tablespoon water. Add cheese and egg mixture to flour. Mix with fingertips. Add remaining water, 1 tablespoon at a time, mixing with fingers until dough is moistened. On floured board knead dough about 10 times. Roll dough to ⅛-inch thickness. Cut into strips about 6 × ½ inch.

Arrange strips on prepared baking sheet. Brush with milk. Bake until light golden brown, 10 to 20 minutes. Remove from baking sheet. Cool on wire rack. Serve with raw vegetables.

Serves 4.

Provolone Puff Pastry

3 sheets frozen puff pastry (each sheet should measure 10 × 9½ × ⅛ inch), defrosted
6 slices (1 oz. each) fully-cooked ham or Prosciutto
12 oz. mild Provolone*, cut into 6 slices
1 egg, beaten
Endive leaves (optional)
Boiled ham slices (optional)

*Remove wax coating from cheese.

Preheat oven to 400°F. Grease large baking sheet. Set aside.

Cut each sheet of pastry into 4 (4½-inch) squares. Arrange 6 squares on prepared baking sheet. Place 1 ham slice in center of each square. Top each with 1 slice of cheese. Brush edges of pastry with egg. Leave edges free.

Roll out remaining pastry into 4 (5-inch) squares. Cover ham and cheese with pastry squares. Crimp edges carefully with tines of fork to seal. Brush tops with remaining egg.

Bake until pastry is golden and puffed, 15 to 25 minutes. Arrange on serving platter. Garnish with endive and rolled slices of ham.

Serves 6 to 8.

Zucchini/Fontina Puff Pastry

1 to 2 small zucchini, peeled and cut into ½-inch slices
2 sheets frozen puff pastry (each sheet should measure 10 × 9½ × ⅛ inch), defrosted
8 oz. Fontina, sliced
1 egg, beaten
1 teaspoon milk

Preheat oven to 425°F. Lightly grease baking sheet. Set aside.

In medium saucepan, heat water to boiling. Add zucchini. Cook about 3 minutes, or until tender-crisp. Drain and arrange zucchini on wire rack to cool.

Roll each sheet of pastry into 10-inch square. Cut each sheet into 20 squares. Place 1 zucchini slice in center of each of 20 squares. Top each with small slice of cheese. In small bowl, blend egg and milk. Brush edges of pastry with egg mixture. Cover with remaining pastry squares. Crimp edges carefully with tines of fork to seal. Arrange on prepared baking sheet. Bake until pastry is golden brown and puffed, about 15 to 20 minutes.

Serves 4.

Bel Paese® Puff Pastry

Serve these turnovers for dinner. Smaller turnovers can be served as hors d'oeuvres.

1½ cups shredded Bel Paese® cheese* (6 oz.)
 3 hard-cooked eggs, peeled and chopped
 ½ cup freshly grated Parmigiano-Reggiano or Grana Padano (about 1 oz.)
 ½ cup thick, homemade tomato sauce or prepared pizza sauce
 2 sheets frozen puff pastry (each sheet should measure 10×9×⅛ inch), defrosted
 1 egg, beaten
 1 tablespoon milk

*Remove wax coating and moist, white crust from cheese.

Preheat oven to 400°F. Grease large baking sheet. Set aside.

In medium mixing bowl, combine Bel Paese®, eggs, Parmigiano-Reggiano and tomato sauce. Set mixture aside.

On lightly floured surface, roll each sheet of pastry into a 13-inch square. Cut each sheet of pastry into 16 squares. In small bowl, combine egg and milk. Brush edges of pastry with egg mixture. Place heaping teaspoonful of cheese mixture in center of each square. Fold each square in half diagonally to form a turnover. Crimp edges carefully with fork tines to seal. Arrange on prepared baking sheet. Bake until puffed and deep golden brown, about 15 to 20 minutes.

Serves 4.

Bel Paese® Puff Pastry

Provolone Teasers

10 oz. mild Provolone*, cut into bite-size cubes
   Cocktail wieners
   Cocktail onions
   Baby dill or gherkin pickles
   Black olives, pitted or pimiento-stuffed olives
 1 grapefruit or other large fruit.

*Remove wax coating from cheese.

Alternate cheese, wieners, onions, pickles and olives on wooden picks, shish kebab style. Serve by piercing grapefruit with kebabs.

Serves 6.

Pastry Shells with Bel Paese® and Mushrooms

8 oz. fresh mushrooms, cleaned
  and sliced
1 clove garlic, minced
3 to 4 tablespoons olive oil
2 teaspoons all-purpose flour
½ cup half-and-half
2 tablespoons minced fresh
  parsley
¼ teaspoon salt
  Dash pepper
4 oz. Bel Paese® cheese*, cut
  into small pieces
8 ready-to-eat pastry shells or
  frozen pastry shells, baked

*Remove wax coating and moist, white crust from cheese.

Preheat oven to 350°F. In small skillet, sauté mushrooms and garlic in olive oil, over medium heat until mushrooms are tender. Stir in flour, half-and-half, parsley, salt and pepper. Remove from heat.

Arrange pastry shells on baking sheet. Line shells with half the cheese. Spoon sauce over cheese. Top with remaining cheese. Bake until cheese melts, 3 to 4 minutes.

Serves 4.

Ready-to-eat pastry shells and frozen shells are available in bakeries or gourmet shops and specialty sections of supermarkets. These shells should not be sweet.

Fontina-Filled Shells

¼ cup butter
2 tablespoons all-purpose flour
¼ teaspoon salt
2 cups milk
⅛ teaspoon ground nutmeg
1 cup shredded Fontina
  (about 3½ oz.)
6 ready-to-eat pastry shells or
  frozen pastry shells, baked
  Fresh parsley sprigs (optional)

Preheat oven to 375°F. In medium saucepan, melt butter. Stir in flour and salt. Blend in milk. Cook over medium heat until thickened, stirring constantly. Add nutmeg and cheese, stirring until cheese melts.

Arrange pastry shells on baking sheet. Fill each shell with cheese sauce. Bake until hot, about 5 minutes. Arrange on serving platter. Garnish with parsley.

Serves 4 to 6.

Pastry Shells with Bel Paese® and Mushrooms

Freshly-Picked Zucchini Flowers with Bel Paese®

Zucchini flowers are a real delicacy and are available during the summer months in Italian food markets. If you have the opportunity to pick your own flowers from zucchini plants, pick only male flowers so the zucchini crop will not be ruined. Female flowers are easily distinguished from the male because the female flowers have the zucchini attached to them and have shorter stems. Be sure to pick the flowers early in the morning while they are still open. When the flowers close, they often trap bees inside.

10 to 15 zucchini flowers
 3 oz. Bel Paese® cheese*, cut
   into 1½ × ¼-inch sticks
   Flour for coating

1 egg, beaten
  Fine dry bread crumbs
  Vegetable oil for frying

*Remove wax coating and moist, white crust from cheese.

Wash zucchini flowers and open one side. Remove filament and stem. Arrange on paper towels to dry.

Place 1 stick cheese in center of each opened flower. Carefully close flower. Roll in flour, then in egg, and finally in bread crumbs. In medium skillet, heat ⅛ inch oil over medium heat. Fry flowers until golden brown and crunchy, turning once. Drain on paper towels. Serve immediately.

Serves 4.

Frankfurter Hors d'oeuvres

3 to 4 oz. Bel Paese® cheese*, cut
   into 8 thin strips
8 strips pimiento bottled in
   olive oil
8 frankfurters, cut in half
   lengthwise
8 slices bacon

*Remove wax coating and moist, white crust from cheese.

Preheat oven to Broil. Place 1 cheese strip and 1 pimiento strip on each of 8 frankfurter halves. Top with remaining frankfurter halves. Wrap 1 bacon slice around each frankfurter sealing in cheese. Pierce with wooden picks to hold. Arrange on broiler pan. Broil about 4 inches from heat, until bacon is crisp, 3 to 5 minutes per side.

Serves 4.

Cabbage/Onion Soup with Provolone

1 small head Savoy cabbage
3 tablespoons butter
1 medium onion, chopped
5 to 6 oz. smoked bacon, cut into small pieces
1 clove garlic, minced
6 cups water
6 beef or chicken bouillon cubes
  Pepper
1 clove garlic, cut in half
8 slices crusty Italian bread, toasted
8 oz. mild Provolone*, cut into 8 slices

*Remove wax coating from cheese.

Remove core and cut cabbage into narrow strips. Set aside.

In large saucepan, melt butter. Add onion, bacon and minced garlic. Cook until light brown. Add cabbage. Mix well and cook about 5 minutes over low heat.

Add water, bouillon cubes and pepper to taste. Heat to boiling. Reduce heat. Cover and cook over low heat until cabbage is tender, about 15 minutes.

Rub slices of bread with garlic halves. Place 2 slices of bread in each individual soup bowl. Top with 2 slices of cheese. Ladle hot soup into bowls.

Serves 4.

Potato Balls in Broth

¾ lb. potatoes
1 cup freshly grated Parmigiano-Reggiano
  (about 3½ oz.)
2 oz. fully-cooked ham, finely chopped (about ½ cup)
2 egg yolks
2 tablespoons butter
⅛ teaspoon ground nutmeg
  Salt
  Flour for coating
  Vegetable oil for frying
3 to 4 cups beef or chicken broth
  Freshly grated Parmigiano-Reggiano

In large saucepan, place potatoes and water to cover. Heat to boiling. Cover and cook over medium-low heat until tender, 20 to 25 minutes. Drain and peel. In medium mixing bowl, mash potatoes. Stir in cheese, ham, egg yolks, butter and nutmeg. Add salt to taste. Mix well to form dough. Shape dough into 1-inch balls. Roll balls in flour.

In medium skillet, heat ⅛ inch oil over medium heat. Fry half the potato balls until golden brown, turning once. Drain on paper towels. Repeat with remaining balls.

Meanwhile in large saucepan, heat broth to boiling. Add potato balls and serve immediately with plenty of Parmigiano-Reggiano.

Serves 4.

Potato Balls in Broth

Grated Parmigiano Crumbs in Broth

Grated Parmigiano Crumbs in Broth

¾ cup freshly grated Parmigiano-Reggiano
  (about 2 oz.)
¾ cup fine dry unseasoned bread crumbs
½ cup all-purpose flour
 2 eggs
 3 to 4 cups beef or chicken broth
   Freshly grated Parmigiano-Reggiano

In medium mixing bowl, stir together cheese, bread crumbs, flour and eggs. Shape into a ball. Using the coarse side of a hand grater, shred the ball onto a large plate. Let cheese mixture dry about 1 hour.

In medium saucepan, heat broth to boiling. Reduce heat to simmer. Add cheese crumbs to broth and cook for 2 to 3 minutes. Serve with Parmigiano-Reggiano.

Serves 4.

Medallion Soup

2 (¾ oz. each) Bel Paese® Process
  Cheese Medallions
1 can (10¾ oz.) condensed cream of tomato, celery
  or potato soup or condensed beef broth
4 cups water
½ cup pastina* or very small macaroni, or
  spaghettini broken into small pieces

In medium mixing bowl, mash the cheese. Set aside.

In medium saucepan, prepare soup according to directions on can. Keep warm. In large saucepan, heat water to boiling. Add pastina and cook until tender but still firm. Drain.

Add a few ladles of soup to the cheese. Mix until cheese melts. Return cheese mixture to saucepan. Stir until cheese and soup are blended and hot. Add pastina. Serve immediately.

Serves 2 to 4.

*Pastina is a very small soup pasta.

Medallion Vegetable Soup

2 cups water
1 carrot, sliced
1 zucchini, sliced
1 tomato, peeled and chopped
¼ teaspoon salt
1 teaspoon pastina (very small soup pasta)
1 (¾ oz.) Bel Paese® Process Cheese Medallion

In small saucepan, combine water, vegetables and salt. Cover and cook over low heat about 1 hour.

Strain vegetable mixture with sieve or press through food mill. Return strained broth and puréed vegetables to saucepan. Heat to boiling. Add pastina and cook until tender.

Mash the cheese in a soup bowl. Slowly stir in soup until cheese melts. Serve hot.

Serves 1.

BABY FOOD VARIATION: Omit salt. Puréed vegetables can be omitted for younger babies.

Onion Soup

1 to 1½ lbs. onions, sliced
    Vegetable oil for frying
1 teaspoon all-purpose flour
4 cups beef broth or beef bouillon
¼ teaspoon salt
⅛ teaspoon pepper
4 slices Italian bread, toasted
4 oz. Bel Paese® cheese*, cut into 4 slices
½ cup freshly grated Parmigiano-Reggiano
    (about 1 oz.)

*Remove wax coating and moist, white crust from cheese.

Preheat oven to 350°F. In large saucepan, sauté onions in oil until golden. Sprinkle with flour and cook an additional 5 minutes. Add broth, salt and pepper. Reduce heat and simmer for 30 minutes.

In each of 4 small ovenproof crocks, place 1 slice toast. Top with 1 slice Bel Paese® and 2 tablespoons Parmigiano-Reggiano. Ladle onion soup into crocks. Bake for 10 minutes. Serve hot.

Serves 4.

Onion Soup

Special Bel Paese® Salad

6 oz. Bel Paese® cheese*, cut
   into small pieces
1 head romaine or 2 heads
   Boston lettuce, rinsed,
   drained and torn into
   bite-size pieces
1 jar (6 oz.) marinated artichoke
   hearts, drained
¼ lb. Milano, Genoa or any
   mild, finely ground salami,
   cubed
¼ lb. Prosciutto, cubed
20 pitted black olives
1 large ripe tomato, cut into
   small wedges
½ cucumber, peeled and sliced
4 scallions or green onions, cut
   into small pieces
1 cup cauliflowerets, cut into
   bite-size pieces
   Italian or other salad dressing

*Remove wax coating and moist,
 white crust from cheese.

In large salad bowl, combine all
ingredients. Season with your
favorite dressing. Toss to coat.

Serves 6 to 8.

Mushroom Salad with Bel Paese®

2 cups sliced fresh mushrooms
3 stalks celery, sliced
4 oz. Bel Paese® cheese*, cut
   into small cubes
3 tablespoons extra virgin
   olive oil
2 tablespoons fresh lemon juice
⅛ teaspoon sugar
   Salt
   Pepper

*Remove wax coating and moist,
 white crust from cheese.

In medium salad bowl, combine
mushrooms, celery and cheese. In
1-cup measure, blend olive oil,
lemon juice and sugar. Add salt
and pepper to taste. Pour over
salad. Toss to coat.

Serves 4.

Special Bel Paese® Salad

Bel Paese® and Macaroni Salad

12 to 14 oz. elbow macaroni, cooked, drained
    and cooled
8 oz. Bel Paese® cheese*, cut into small cubes
3 large ripe tomatoes, chopped
3 stalks celery, chopped
⅓ cup finely chopped onion
2 tablespoons mayonnaise
¼ teaspoon salt
⅛ teaspoon pepper
    Fresh parsley sprigs (optional)

*Remove wax coating and moist, white crust
from cheese.

In large salad bowl, combine all ingredients.
Toss to coat. Garnish with parsley.

Serves 4.

Fontina, Taleggio, Caciotta or any mild sheep's milk
table cheese can be substituted for Bel Paese®.

Raw Zucchini Salad with Grated Parmigiano

Raw Zucchini Salad with Grated Parmigiano

2 medium zucchini, cut into thin slices
1 large ripe tomato, cut into eighths, or 6 cherry
    tomatoes, each cut in half
1 carrot, cut into small pieces
⅓ cup finely chopped onion
¼ cup Italian salad dressing
3 to 4 tablespoons freshly grated
    Parmigiano-Reggiano
    Lettuce leaves (optional)

In medium mixing bowl, toss all ingredients. Let
stand at room temperature at least 1 hour to
marinate. Stir occasionally. Place in lettuce-lined
salad bowl.

Serves 4 to 6.

Marinated Artichoke Salad with Prosciutto and Grana Padano

1 jar (6 oz.) marinated artichoke hearts, drained (reserve liquid)
2 cups small shell or elbow macaroni, cooked, drained and cooled
3 oz. Prosciutto, cubed
¾ cup freshly grated Grana Padano (about 2 oz.)
2 tablespoons minced fresh parsley
2 large fresh basil leaves, cut into small pieces

Cut artichoke hearts into small pieces. In large salad bowl, combine all ingredients. Add enough reserved liquid from artichokes to moisten salad. Toss to coat.

Serves 4.

Red Cabbage Salad

1 small head red cabbage, shredded
8 oz. Bel Paese® cheese*, cut into small chunks
1 cup thinly sliced celery hearts
2 oz. fully-cooked ham, cut into small chunks (about ½ cup)
3 to 5 tablespoons mayonnaise
3 to 5 teaspoons fresh lemon juice

*Remove wax coating and moist, white crust from cheese.

In large salad bowl, combine all ingredients. Toss to coat.

Serves 4 to 6.

Red Cabbage Salad

Chicken Salad with Provolone

2 whole chicken breasts, cooked and sliced
1 potato, cooked, peeled and thinly sliced
1 beet, cooked, peeled and sliced
2 carrots, cut into thin strips
1 stalk celery heart, cut into small pieces
1 fennel plant, cut into small pieces
½ cup extra virgin olive oil
2 tablespoons fresh lemon juice
¼ teaspoon salt
1 fresh parsley sprig, minced
1 Delicious apple, cubed
5½ oz. mild Provolone*, cut into large cubes
1 cup chopped walnuts
   Mayonnaise

*Remove wax coating from cheese.

Prepare chicken. Set aside. Prepare each vegetable separately; keep in individual bowls. In 1-cup measure, blend olive oil, lemon juice and salt. Season each vegetable with olive oil mixture. Add parsley to potato slices. Sprinkle apple with olive oil mixture.

Place chicken slices in center of large serving platter. Arrange seasoned vegetables, apple, cheese and walnuts in small mounds around chicken. Serve with mayonnaise.

Serves 4 to 6.

Rice Salad with Toscanello

Salad
2½ cups cooked brown or white rice, rinsed, drained and cooled
1 can (6½ oz.) tuna, drained and flaked
4 frankfurters, boiled and cut into small pieces
3 hard-cooked eggs, peeled and chopped
2 to 3 oz. roasted peppers bottled in oil, drained
2 medium ripe tomatoes, cut into quarters
4 oz. Toscanello, cut into small chunks
1 or 2 gherkin pickles, sliced
12 black olives, pitted and minced

Dressing
3 tablespoons extra virgin olive oil
1 tablespoon fresh lemon juice
¼ teaspoon salt
   Dash pepper
   Lettuce leaves (optional)

In large salad bowl, combine all salad ingredients. Toss gently. In 1-cup measure, blend all dressing ingredients. Pour over salad. Toss to coat. Serve salad on lettuce-lined platter.

Serves 4 as a main dish or 6 to 8 as a side dish.

Caciotta or any mild sheep's milk table cheese can be substituted for Toscanello.

Chicken Salad with Provolone

Melted Provolone in Tomato Sauce

2 cloves garlic, minced
3 tablespoons extra virgin olive oil
1 can (16 oz.) crushed tomatoes or 1 can (16 oz.)
   whole tomatoes, chopped
½ teaspoon dried basil leaves
   Salt
   Pepper
1 lb. mild Provolone*, cut into 8 slices
¼ teaspoon dried oregano leaves

*Remove wax coating from cheese.

In large skillet, sauté garlic in olive oil over medium-high heat for a few seconds. Add tomatoes and basil. Season with salt and pepper. Reduce heat and simmer about 15 minutes, stirring occasionally.

Arrange cheese slices on tomatoes. Sprinkle with oregano. Cover and cook over low heat until cheese begins to melt, about 5 minutes. Serve with a fresh garden salad and Italian bread.

Serves 4.

Fried Fontina Sticks

1 cup all-purpose flour
2 eggs
½ cup dry white wine
8 oz. Fontina, cut into 3 × 1½ × ¼-inch sticks
   Flour for coating
   Vegetable oil for frying

Preheat oven to 150°F.

In large mixing bowl, combine flour, eggs and wine. Stir until well mixed. In plastic bag, shake cheese sticks and small amount of flour to coat. Add Fontina sticks to batter.

In large skillet, heat ⅛ inch oil over medium-high heat. Use a spoon to remove a few cheese sticks from batter. Fry cheese sticks until light golden brown, 20 to 30 seconds, turning once. Remove from skillet with slotted spoon. Drain on paper towels. Place in baking dish and keep warm in oven until all cheese sticks are fried. Serve with garden salad or side dish of vegetables.

Serves 2 to 3.

Fried Fontina Sticks

Bel Paese® "Cutlets"

Croque Madame Bel Paese®

2 tablespoons butter
2 tablespoons all-purpose flour
⅔ cup milk
¾ cup freshly grated Grana Padano (about 1½ oz.)
4 slices bread
4 slices Prosciutto
8 oz. Bel Paese® cheese*, cut into 8 slices
   Ground nutmeg (freshy grated, if available)

*Remove wax coating and moist, white crust
 from cheese.

Preheat oven to 400°F. In small saucepan, melt butter. Stir in flour. Blend in milk. Cook over medium-low heat until sauce thickens, stirring constantly. Add Grana Padano. Stir until sauce is smooth.

Spread 1 side of each slice of bread with cheese sauce. Arrange in 9-inch square baking dish, plain side down. Place 1 slice Prosciutto and 2 slices Bel Paese® on each slice of bread. Sprinkle with nutmeg. Bake for 5 to 10 minutes. Serve hot.

Serves 4.

Bel Paese® "Cutlets"

The "cutlets" can be coated in advance, then refrigerated until ready to fry and serve. A light red wine will complement this dish nicely.

2 eggs
⅛ teaspoon pepper
8 oz. Bel Paese® cheese*, cut into 8 slices
1 cup fine dry bread crumbs
   Vegetable oil for frying

*Remove wax coating and moist, white crust
 from cheese.

In small bowl, beat eggs and pepper. Dip each cheese slice in egg, then roll in bread crumbs. Dip again in egg and bread crumbs, being careful not to loosen first layer of coating.

In large skillet, heat ⅛ inch oil over medium heat. Fry 4 cheese slices until golden brown, 1½ to 2 minutes, turning once. Drain on paper towels. Repeat with remaining cheese.

Serves 2.

Provolone "Cutlets"

½ cup fine dry bread crumbs
2 teaspoons dried rosemary leaves
2 teaspoons minced fresh sage leaves or
   1 teaspoon ground sage
2 teaspoons minced fresh thyme leaves or
   1 teaspoon ground thyme
1 clove garlic, minced
2 eggs
   Salt
   Pepper
1 lb. mild Provolone*, cut into 8 slices
   Butter or margarine for frying

*Remove wax coating from cheese.

In small bowl, mix bread crumbs, rosemary, sage, thyme and garlic. In another small bowl, beat eggs. Add salt and pepper to taste. Dip each cheese slice in egg, then roll in bread crumbs, coating well.

In large skillet, melt small amount of butter over medium heat. Fry cheese slices until golden brown, turning once. Drain on paper towels. Repeat with remaining cheese. Do not overcook because the cheese will melt. Serve the "cutlets" with a garden salad or boiled potatoes.

Serves 4.

Seared Provolone Slices with Herb Dressing

Fresh herbs are preferable, but dried herbs can be substituted.

Herb Dressing

- 3 tablespoons extra virgin olive oil
- 2 tablespoons fresh lemon juice
- 1 fresh parsley sprig, minced, or 1 teaspoon dried parsley flakes
- 1 fresh rosemary sprig, minced, or ½ teaspoon dried rosemary leaves
- 3 or 4 fresh sage leaves, minced, or ¼ teaspoon ground sage
- 2 cloves garlic, pressed
- ⅛ teaspoon salt
- ⅛ teaspoon pepper

- 1¼ lbs. mild Provolone*, cut into 8 equal slices

*Remove wax coating from cheese.

In small bowl, combine Herb Dressing ingredients. Stir vigorously with fork until well mixed. Set aside.

Heat large non-stick skillet over medium-high heat until a drop of water beads up on surface. Arrange 4 slices of cheese in skillet. Cook until cheese is seared and begins to melt around edges, turning over after a few seconds. (The outside of the cheese will sear and not stick to the skillet.) Repeat with remaining cheese.

Arrange cheese slices on large platter. Sprinkle with Herb Dressing. Serve with Italian bread and a garden salad.

Serves 4.

Golden Brown Provolone Sandwiches with Tomato Sauce

Golden Brown Provolone Sandwiches with Tomato Sauce

- 12 oz. mild Provolone*, cut into 6 slices
- 12 slices white bread
- 3 eggs, beaten
- Salt
- White pepper
- Flour for coating
- Fine dry bread crumbs for coating
- ¼ cup vegetable oil
- 2 tablespoons butter
- Endive leaves (optional)
- 2 cups warm homemade tomato sauce or prepared pizza sauce

*Remove wax coating from cheese.

Place each slice of cheese between 2 slices of bread. Trim bread to size and shape of the cheese.

In shallow bowl, blend eggs, salt and white pepper. Dip each sandwich in egg, then roll in flour. Dip again in egg and then roll in bread crumbs, pressing to coat all sides.

In large skillet, heat oil and butter over medium heat. Fry sandwiches until golden brown, turning once. Drain on paper towels. Arrange on serving plate and garnish with endive leaves. Serve with tomato sauce.

Serves 6.

Taleggio Supper Sandwiches

Taleggio Supper Sandwiches

6 oz. Taleggio*
2 tablespoons butter, softened
⅛ teaspoon dry mustard
8 thin slices Italian bread, cut
    into 2 × 1-inch strips
2 eggs, beaten
2 teaspoons milk
    Flour for coating
    Vegetable or olive oil for frying
    Tomato sauce (optional)

*Remove wax coating and moist,
 white crust from cheese.

Allow Taleggio to soften at room
temperature for 30 minutes. In
small bowl, mix cheese, butter
and mustard. Spread mixture on
1 side of half the bread strips. Top
with remaining bread strips to
make small sandwiches. In shallow
bowl, blend eggs and milk. Roll
each sandwich in flour. Dip in egg
mixture and roll in flour to coat.

In small skillet, heat ⅛ inch oil
over medium heat. Fry sandwiches
until golden brown, turning once.
Drain on paper towels. Serve warm
tomato sauce over sandwiches.
Serve with a fresh garden salad.

Serves 4.

Stuffed Torpedo Rolls

2 torpedo rolls
2 tablespoons milk
1 frankfurter, sliced
2 to 3 tablespoons freshly
    grated Grana Padano
1 oz. Bel Paese® cheese*,
    cut into small pieces
1 egg yolk, beaten
1 tablespoon butter, melted
1 teaspoon white wine
¼ teaspoon ground sage
    Salt
    Pepper

*Remove wax coating and moist,
 white crust from cheese.

Preheat oven to 350°F. Butter
12 × 8-inch baking dish. Set aside.

Cut each roll in half lengthwise
and remove soft bread from each
half. In medium mixing bowl,
combine soft bread pieces and
milk. Add frankfurter, Grana
Padano, Bel Paese®, egg yolk,
butter, wine and sage. Mix well.
Add salt and pepper to taste.

Spoon mixture into each roll.
Arrange rolls in prepared baking
dish. Bake until cheese melts and
bread is toasted, about 10 minutes.

Serves 2.

Grilled Bel Paese® and Tuna

1 can (6½ oz.) tuna, drained
    and flaked
2 tablespoons mayonnaise or
    plain yogurt
    Butter
6 slices white or
    whole wheat bread
2 to 3 oz. Bel Paese® cheese*,
    cut into 6 slices
    Tomato slices (optional)

*Remove wax coating and moist,
 white crust from cheese.

In small bowl, mix tuna and
mayonnaise. Set aside.

Lightly butter 1 side of each slice
of bread. In large skillet or on
griddle, place 3 slices of bread,
buttered-side down. Place 1 slice
of cheese on each slice of bread.
Spread with tuna mixture. Top
with remaining cheese slices.
Cover with remaining bread,
buttered-side up. Fry sandwiches
over medium heat until golden
brown and cheese melts, turning
once. Serve hot with tomato slices.

Serves 3.

Mortadella with Bel Paese®

1 slice (about ½ inch thick)
   Bel Paese® cheese*
2 slices (each about ¼ inch thick)
   Mortadella
1 egg, beaten
¼ cup fine dry bread crumbs
   Vegetable oil for frying

*Remove wax coating and moist,
 white crust from cheese.

Place the cheese between slices of
Mortadella. Dip in egg, then roll
in bread crumbs. Dip again in egg
and bread crumbs.

In small skillet, heat ⅛ inch oil
over medium heat. Fry until
golden brown, 2½ to 3 minutes,
turning once. Serve immediately.

Serves 1 hearty appetite.

Bel Paese® Toast

2 slices white or whole
   wheat bread
   Butter
1 slice (1 to 2 oz.)
   Bel Paese® cheese*
1 slice Prosciutto

*Remove wax coating and moist,
 white crust from cheese.

Preheat toaster oven to 350°F.
Butter 1 side of each slice of
bread. Place cheese and Prosciutto
between plain sides of bread.
Bake in toaster oven until cheese
melts, 5 to 10 minutes.

To prepare in microwave oven:
Toast bread first. Omit butter.
Top 1 slice of toast with cheese
and Prosciutto. Place on paper
towel in microwave oven.
Microwave at HIGH for 30 to 45
seconds, or until cheese melts.
Top with remaining toast. Serve
immediately.

Serves 1.

Ham and Cheese Omelette

Ham and Cheese Omelette

4 eggs
1 tablespoon milk
4 to 5 tablespoons freshly grated
   Parmigiano-Reggiano or
   Grana Padano

Butter or margarine for frying
4 thin slices Prosciutto or
   fully-cooked ham
4 thin slices Bel Paese® cheese*

*Remove wax coating and moist, white crust from cheese.

In medium mixing bowl, beat eggs and milk well. Stir in Parmigiano-
Reggiano. In large skillet, melt butter over medium heat. Add enough
egg mixture to thinly cover bottom of skillet. Cook until just set.

Place 1 slice of Prosciutto and 1 slice Bel Paese® on omelette. Carefully
roll up omelette with Prosciutto and Bel Paese® inside. With seam-side
of omelette down, reduce heat to medium-low. Cook until cheese
melts, 1 to 2 minutes. Repeat with remaining egg mixture, Prosciutto
and Bel Paese® to make 4 omelettes.

Serves 4.

Prosciutto will give a saltier taste to the omelette.

Cheese Covered Omelette

2 eggs
1 tablespoon milk
1 tablespoon butter or margarine
¼ cup chopped onion

4 oz. Bel Paese® cheese*,
   thinly sliced
   Dash pepper
¼ teaspoon dried oregano leaves

*Remove wax coating and moist, white crust from cheese.

In small bowl, beat eggs and milk. Set aside. In medium skillet, sauté
onion in butter over medium heat, until tender. Add egg mixture. Cook
until golden brown on bottom, then turn over. Top with cheese.
Sprinkle with pepper and oregano. Cover and reduce heat to
medium-low. Cook until cheese melts. Serve immediately.

Serves 1 to 2.

Belgian Eggs

This recipe is excellent for brunch or a light luncheon.

1 tablespoon butter, melted
4 slices white or whole wheat
    bread, toasted and buttered
4 slices Grana Padano
4 egg whites
4 egg yolks (for ease of handling,
    keep each yolk in its own dish)
2 tablespoons freshly grated
    Grana Padano

Preheat oven to 350°F. Brush 9-inch square baking dish with melted butter. Arrange toast in prepared dish. Place 1 slice of cheese on each slice of toast.

In medium mixing bowl, beat egg whites at high speed of electric mixer until stiff. Spoon a mound of egg whites onto each slice of cheese. Make a well in center of each mound. Place an egg yolk in each well. Sprinkle each egg yolk with grated cheese. Bake until eggs are set, about 15 minutes.

Serves 4.

Eggs with Bel Paese® and Prosciutto

2 tablespoons butter or margarine
1 tablespoon vegetable oil
2 thin slices Prosciutto
3 eggs
1 oz. Bel Paese® cheese*,
    chopped

*Remove wax coating and moist, white crust from cheese.

In medium skillet, heat butter and oil over medium heat. Add Prosciutto and brown lightly, turning once. Add eggs to skillet over Prosciutto. Sprinkle with cheese. Continue to cook until eggs are desired doneness and cheese melts. Serve immediately.

Serves 1 hearty appetite.

Belgian Eggs

Little Stuffed Omelettes with Bel Paese®

6 eggs
1 tablespoon milk
2 tablespoons minced fresh parsley or 2 teaspoons
   dried parsley flakes
¼ teaspoon salt
⅛ teaspoon pepper
   Butter or margarine for frying
2 slices fully-cooked ham or Prosciutto, cut in half
2 oz. Bel Paese® cheese*, cut into 4 slices

*Remove wax coating and moist, white crust
from cheese.

Preheat oven to 150°F. In medium mixing bowl, beat
eggs, milk, parsley, salt and pepper. In small skillet,
melt small amount of butter over medium heat. Add
⅓ cup egg mixture to skillet. Cook until bottom of
omelette is golden brown, turning once. In center of
each omelette, place half slice of ham and 1 slice of
cheese. Fold sides of omelette over ham and cheese.
Arrange in 9-inch baking dish and place in oven to
keep warm. Repeat to make 4 omelettes.

Serves 4.

Scrambled Eggs with Bel Paese®

1 tablespoon vegetable oil
1 tablespoon butter
1 tablespoon chopped onion
1 large ripe tomato, seeded and chopped
2 to 3 fresh basil leaves, minced
3 eggs
⅛ teaspoon salt
⅛ teaspoon pepper
3 to 4 oz. Bel Paese® cheese*, chopped
¼ cup freshly grated Parmigiano-Reggiano

*Remove wax coating and moist, white crust
from cheese.

In large skillet, heat oil and butter over medium
heat. Add onion and sauté until transparent. Add
tomato. Reduce heat and simmer for 10 minutes.
Add basil and cook 5 minutes.

Add eggs, salt and pepper to skillet. Beat eggs and
tomato mixture with fork. Cook until eggs are set,
but still moist. Sprinkle with Bel Paese® and
Parmigiano-Reggiano. Cover and cook over low heat
until eggs are desired doneness and cheese melts.

Serves 2.

Little Stuffed Omelettes with Bel Paese®

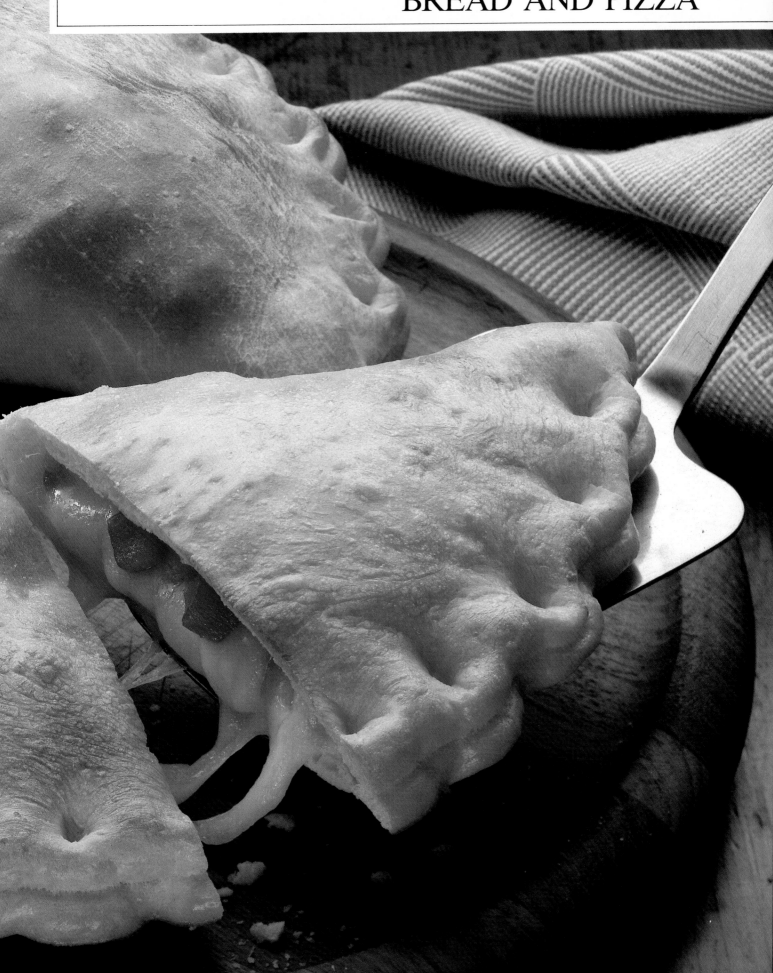

Provolone Pizza Toast

4 slices dry, crusty Italian bread
1 clove garlic, cut in half
½ cup homemade tomato sauce
    or prepared pizza sauce
4 fresh basil leaves, minced or
    1 teaspoon dried basil leaves
4 anchovy fillets, minced
    Salt
    Pepper
2 cups shredded mild Provolone*
    (8 oz.)
    Extra virgin olive oil

*Remove wax coating from cheese.

Preheat oven to 375°F. Grease baking sheet.

Rub slices of bread with garlic halves. Place bread on prepared baking sheet. Top each slice of bread with 2 tablespoons tomato sauce, basil and anchovy. Sprinkle lightly with salt and pepper. Sprinkle with cheese. Drizzle with olive oil. Bake until cheese is melted, 5 to 10 minutes.

Serves 4.

Bel Paese® Pizza Toast

1 slice Italian bread or half an
    English muffin, buttered
1 thin slice Prosciutto
1 slice Bel Paese® cheese*
    Dash dried oregano leaves
1 pitted black olive, sliced

*Remove wax coating and moist, white crust from cheese.

Preheat oven to 350°F. Top buttered bread with Prosciutto and cheese. Sprinkle with oregano and olive. Place on baking sheet. Bake until cheese begins to melt, about 5 minutes.

To prepare in microwave oven: Toast bread. Omit butter. Assemble sandwich. Place on paper towel in microwave oven. Microwave at HIGH for about 30 seconds, or until cheese melts.

Serves 1.

Provolone Pizza Toast

Bel Paese® English Muffin Pizza

2 English muffins, split
  and toasted
¼ cup homemade tomato sauce
  or prepared pizza sauce
⅛ teaspoon pepper
½ teaspoon dried parsley flakes
  Anchovy fillets, minced
8 oz. Bel Paese® cheese*, cut
  into 4 slices

*Remove wax coating and moist,
 white crust from cheese.

Preheat oven to 350°F. Arrange
muffin halves in 9-inch baking
dish. Spread 1 tablespoon tomato
sauce on each muffin half.
Sprinkle each with pepper, parsley
flakes and anchovies. Top each
muffin half with a slice of cheese.
Bake until cheese melts, 15 to
20 minutes.

To prepare in microwave oven:
Toast muffins first. Assemble
pizzas. Place on paper towels in
microwave oven. Microwave at
HIGH for 1 to 3 minutes, or until
cheese melts.

Serve with a garden salad.

Serves 2.

Bel Paese® English Muffin Pizza

Bel Paese®/Prosciutto Calzone

Bel Paese®/Prosciutto Calzone pictured on page 92.

Calzone is a pizza which is folded in half, resembling a turnover
in shape.

Pizza Dough
1 pkg. active dry yeast
1⅓ cups warm water
  (105° to 115°F)
4 cups sifted all-purpose flour
1 teaspoon salt
2 tablespoons extra virgin
  olive oil

Filling
8 oz. Bel Paese® cheese*,
  cut into small cubes
6 oz. Prosciutto, cubed

1 egg, slightly beaten

*Remove wax coating and moist, white crust from cheese.

In 2-cup measure, dissolve yeast in warm water. In large mixing bowl,
combine flour and salt. Add yeast mixture and oil. Mix well. Knead
dough on floured surface until smooth, about 10 minutes. Shape dough
into a ball. Place in greased bowl. Turn to coat. Cover and let rise in
warm place until double, about 1½ to 2 hours.

Preheat oven to 450°F. Grease baking sheet. Set aside.

Punch down dough. Knead dough on floured surface a few times.
Divide dough into three equal pieces. Shape each piece into a ball. Roll
out each piece into 10-inch circle.

Place cheese and Prosciutto in center of each circle. Fold each circle in
half. Press edges together with fingers to seal. Place on prepared baking
sheet and brush with egg. Bake until deep golden brown, 15 to 20
minutes. Serve immediately.

Serves 4 to 6.

Parmigiano-Reggiano Cheese Bread

1 pkg. active dry yeast
¼ cup warm water
    (105° to 115°F)
4½ cups all-purpose flour
½ cup freshly grated
    Parmigiano-Reggiano or
    Grana Padano
⅓ cup instant nonfat dry milk
2 tablespoons sugar
2 teaspoons salt
1 egg, slightly beaten
1¼ cups warm water
    (105° to 115°F)
2 tablespoons vegetable oil

In small bowl, dissolve yeast in ¼ cup warm water. In large mixing bowl, combine flour, cheese, dry milk, sugar and salt. In small mixing bowl, combine egg, 1¼ cups warm water and oil. Stir yeast mixture and egg mixture into dry ingredients. Mix well. Knead on floured surface until smooth and elastic, about 10 minutes. Shape dough into a ball. Place in greased bowl. Turn dough to coat. Cover and let rise in warm place until double, about 1½ hours.

Grease 9 × 5-inch loaf pan. Set pan aside.

Punch down dough. Shape into a loaf. Place in prepared pan. Cover and let rise until double, 30 to 45 minutes.

Preheat oven to 375°F. Bake until loaf is deep golden brown and sounds hollow when tapped, 35 to 40 minutes. Remove from pan. Cool on wire rack.

Makes 1 loaf.

Gorgonzola Bread

½ cup all-purpose flour
1⅔ cups milk
4 oz. Gorgonzola, cut into
    small pieces
2 eggs, beaten
8 slices white bread

Preheat oven to 375°F. Place flour in medium saucepan. Blend in milk. Cook over medium-low heat until mixture thickens, stirring constantly. Add cheese, stirring constantly until cheese melts. Remove from heat. Stir small amount of hot mixture into eggs. Stir eggs into hot mixture. Mix well until sauce is smooth and easy to spread. Cool.

Place bread on baking sheet. Spread about ¼ cup sauce on 1 side of each slice of bread. Bake until puffed and lightly browned, 10 to 15 minutes.

Serves 4.

Gorgonzola Biscuits

7 oz. Gorgonzola
1 cup all-purpose flour
6 tablespoons butter, softened
2 egg yolks
⅛ teaspoon salt
⅛ teaspoon pepper
⅛ teaspoon ground nutmeg

Allow Gorgonzola to soften at room temperature for 30 minutes. In medium mixing bowl, combine all ingredients. Mix well. Shape dough into a ball. Cover and refrigerate at least 30 minutes.

Preheat oven to 350°F. Roll out dough on floured surface to ¼-inch thickness. Cut dough into 3-inch circles using top of large glass or sharp knife. Arrange biscuits on baking sheet. Bake until light golden brown, about 10 minutes.

Serves 4.

Parmigiano Buttermilk Biscuits

Try this tasty version of old-fashioned buttermilk biscuits. They are delicious with ham, Prosciutto or a fresh garden salad. Biscuits are best when served right from the oven, but are also good the next day.

The secret of good biscuits is not to overmix the dough, but to stir just until the dough is moist and a few lumps remain.

2 cups all-purpose flour
1 cup freshly grated Parmigiano-Reggiano (about 2 oz.)
1 tablespoon baking powder
½ teaspoon salt
½ teaspoon baking soda
¼ teaspoon freshly ground pepper
3 tablespoons butter or margarine, cut into ¼-inch pieces
1 cup buttermilk

Preheat oven to 400°F. Lightly grease baking sheet. Set aside.

In large mixing bowl, mix flour, cheese, baking powder, salt, baking soda and pepper. Add butter pieces and blend in with fingertips. Add buttermilk, stirring with a wooden spoon or fork until dough is moistened.

Knead dough on floured surface until just smooth, about 10 times. Gently roll out dough into 12 × 9-inch rectangle. Cut dough into 3 × ¾-inch "fingers." Place on prepared baking sheet. Bake until golden brown, 10 to 15 minutes.

Serves 4 to 6.

Parmigiano-Reggiano Cheese Bread

Provolone Pizza

This unique pizza consists of Provolone, bacon and a vegetable inside two layers of pizza crust.

    1 pkg. active dry yeast
    1 cup warm water (105° to 115°F)
 2½ cups all-purpose flour
    ⅛ teaspoon salt
    3 cups shredded mild Provolone* (12 oz.)
    6 slices bacon, cooked and crumbled
    ½ cup chopped, parboiled carrots, spinach or escarole

*Remove wax coating from cheese.

In small bowl, dissolve yeast in warm water. In large mixing bowl, combine flour and salt. Stir in yeast mixture. Knead dough on floured surface until smooth and elastic, 5 to 10 minutes, adding more flour as necessary. Shape dough into a ball. Place in greased bowl. Turn to coat. Cover and let rise in warm place about 1 hour.

Preheat oven to 400°F. Grease 12-inch pizza pan or baking sheet.

Punch down dough. Divide in half. On floured surface, roll out one half into 12-inch circle. Place dough in prepared pan. Sprinkle with half the cheese. Sprinkle with bacon and carrot. Top with remaining cheese. Roll out remaining dough into 12-inch circle. Cover pizza toppings with dough. Seal edges of dough with tines of fork. Bake until golden brown, about 40 minutes.

Serves 4 to 6.

Ham and Gorgonzola Pizza

Dough

    1 pkg. active dry yeast
 1⅓ cups warm water
        (105° to 115°F)
    4 cups sifted all-purpose flour
    1 teaspoon salt
    2 tablespoons extra virgin
        olive oil

Topping

 6 oz. Gorgonzola, sliced
 6 oz. fully-cooked ham,
        thinly sliced
    Salt
    Pepper
 1 tablespoon extra virgin
        olive oil

In 2-cup measure, dissolve yeast in warm water. In large mixing bowl, combine flour and salt. Add yeast mixture and oil. Mix well. Knead dough on floured surface until smooth, about 10 minutes. Shape dough into a ball. Place in greased bowl. Turn to coat. Cover and let rise in warm place until double, 1½ to 2 hours.

Grease baking sheet. Punch down dough. Spread dough on baking sheet into 15 × 12-inch rectangle. Let rise for 15 minutes.

Preheat oven to 400°F. Arrange cheese and ham on dough. Sprinkle with salt and pepper. Sprinkle with olive oil. Bake until crust is golden brown, 25 to 30 minutes. Serve immediately.

Serves 4.

Provolone Pizza

Asparagus Pie

To save time use either a pie crust mix or a frozen pie shell.

Crust
  1 cup all-purpose flour
  ⅛ teaspoon salt
  5 tablespoons butter, cut into
       small pieces
  3 to 5 tablespoons cold water

Filling
  1 lb. asparagus, trimmed
  2 tablespoons butter, melted
  6 oz. Bel Paese® cheese*,
       cut into small pieces
  3 eggs
1¼ cups milk
  ⅛ teaspoon salt

*Remove wax coating and moist, white crust from cheese.

For crust, combine flour and salt on a board. Make a well in center. Add butter pieces to well. Mix flour and butter with fingertips. Add water, 1 tablespoon at a time. Mix well with fingers. Shape into a ball. Cover and let dough rest for 30 minutes.

Meanwhile, cook asparagus in boiling salted water until tender-crisp, about 5 minutes. Drain and cut into 1-inch pieces. Toss with melted butter.

Preheat oven to 350°F. Grease 9-inch pie plate. Set aside. Roll out dough on floured board. Ease dough into pie plate. Trim and flute edge. Pierce bottom of crust several times with fork. Bake for 5 minutes.

Sprinkle asparagus in bottom of pie crust. Sprinkle cheese over asparagus. In medium mixing bowl, beat eggs, milk and salt. Pour into pie crust. Bake until set and golden brown, 40 to 50 minutes.

Serves 3 as a main dish or 6 as a side dish.

Asparagus with Medallion Mornay Sauce

Asparagus with Medallion Mornay Sauce

  ¼ cup butter
  ¼ cup all-purpose flour
  ¾ teaspoon salt
2½ cups milk
  3 (¾ oz. each) Bel Paese®
       Process Cheese Medallions,
       cut into small pieces
  1 lb. asparagus, trimmed

In medium saucepan, melt butter. Stir in flour and salt. Blend in milk. Cook over medium-low heat, until thick and bubbly, stirring constantly. Add cheese. Stir until melted.

In large skillet, heat ½ inch water to boiling. Add asparagus. Cover and cook over medium heat until tender. Drain.

Pour sauce over asparagus. Serve immediately.

Serves 4 to 6.

Cooked broccoli, carrots or cauliflower can be substituted for asparagus.

Asparagus with Béchamel Sauce

  1 lb. asparagus, trimmed
1¾ cups shredded Bel Paese®
       cheese* (6 oz.)
  ¾ cup freshly grated
       Parmigiano-Reggiano (2 oz.)
  1 recipe Béchamel Sauce,
       page 66 (¾ cup)

*Remove wax coating and moist, white crust from cheese.

Preheat oven to 350°F. Grease 1½-quart baking dish. Set aside.

Cook asparagus until tender-crisp. Drain. Cut into pieces. Layer half the asparagus, a third of the Bel Paese® and half the Béchamel Sauce in prepared baking dish. Repeat layers. Top with remaining Bel Paese®. Sprinkle with Parmigiano-Reggiano. Bake until hot and bubbly, about 10 minutes.

Serves 4 to 6.

Peppers Stuffed with Bel Paese® and Chopped Meat

Peppers Stuffed with Bel Paese® and Chopped Meat

4 large green peppers
1 to 2 oz. beef sirloin, cut into ¼-inch cubes
    (3 to 6 tablespoons)
2 tablespoons extra virgin olive oil
3 cups cooked rice
4 oz. Bel Paese® cheese*, cut into small cubes
½ teaspoon dried oregano leaves
⅛ teaspoon salt
⅛ teaspoon pepper
1 egg, beaten
2 oz. Bel Paese® cheese*, cut into 4 slices

*Remove wax coating and moist, white crust
 from cheese.

Preheat oven to 350°F. Cut off stem end and remove
seeds from peppers. Set aside.

In small skillet, brown beef in olive oil over medium
heat. Add rice, cheese cubes, oregano, salt, pepper
and egg. Mix well. Divide mixture and fill each
pepper. Arrange in 9-inch square baking dish. Place
slice of cheese on each pepper. Bake until peppers
are tender, 30 to 45 minutes.

Serves 4.

Parmigiano Stuffed Peppers

4 medium green peppers
¼ lb. sausage
¼ lb. beef sirloin, cut into ¼-inch cubes
¼ cup chopped onion
1½ cups soft fresh bread crumbs
1 egg, beaten
1 tablespoon vegetable oil
1 tablespoon milk
1 teaspoon dried basil leaves
⅛ teaspoon ground nutmeg
4 oz. Parmigiano-Reggiano or Grana Padano,
    cut into 4 slices

Preheat oven to 350°F. Cut off stem end and remove
seeds from peppers. Set aside.

In medium skillet, brown sausage and beef lightly.
Add onion. Cook until tender. Remove from heat.
Drain thoroughly. Add bread crumbs, egg, vegetable
oil, milk, basil and nutmeg.

Divide mixture and fill each pepper. Arrange in
9-inch square baking dish. Cover with foil. Bake for
30 to 45 minutes. Uncover. Place slice of cheese on
each pepper. Continue baking until cheese melts, 10
to 15 minutes. Serve immediately.

Serves 4.

Peppers with Gorgonzola Sauce

3 to 4 oz. Gorgonzola
4 large green peppers, skin removed
⅔ cup half-and-half

Allow Gorgonzola to soften at room temperature for 30 minutes.

To remove skin from peppers, follow one of the following procedures:

1. Broil pepper halves, skin side up on broiler pan about 4 inches from heat for 15 to 20 minutes. Plunge peppers into cold water. Remove skin with a sharp knife.
2. Cook peppers over a gas flame using a long-handled fork, turning frequently until skin blackens. Plunge peppers into cold water. Remove skin with a sharp knife.

Discard skin. Rinse and remove seeds from peppers. Cut peppers into small pieces.

In small bowl, mix cheese and half-and-half until smooth. In medium saucepan, combine peppers and cheese mixture. Cook over medium heat until hot, about 5 minutes.

Serves 4 to 6.

Zucchini Casserole with Bel Paese®

3 to 4 medium zucchini, cut lengthwise into ¼-inch slices
4 to 5 oz. Bel Paese® cheese*, thinly sliced
2 to 3 large ripe tomatoes, chopped or 1 can (16 oz.) whole tomatoes, drained and chopped
2 to 3 fresh basil leaves, minced or ½ teaspoon dried basil leaves

*Remove wax coating and moist, white crust from cheese.

Sprinkle zucchini with salt. Let stand about 1 hour. Rinse with cold water. Dry with paper towels.

Preheat oven to 350°F.

Arrange half the zucchini in 9-inch square baking dish. Cover with half the cheese slices. Top with half the tomatoes and basil. Repeat layers. Bake until zucchini is tender, about 30 minutes.

Serves 4.

Baked Tomatoes with Bel Paese®

3 to 4 large ripe tomatoes, cut into halves
1 to 2 oz. Bel Paese® cheese*, cut into small cubes
2 anchovy fillets, mashed
1 tablespoon capers
2 to 3 fresh parsley sprigs, minced
1 tablespoon extra virgin olive oil

*Remove wax coating and moist, white crust from cheese.

Preheat oven to 350°F. Grease 12 × 8-inch baking dish.

Remove tomato pulp, discard seeds and juice. Chop pulp. Arrange tomato halves in prepared baking dish.

In small mixing bowl, combine tomato pulp, cheese, anchovies, capers and parsley. Fill tomato halves with tomato/cheese mixture. Drizzle olive oil over tomatoes. Bake until tomatoes are hot, 20 to 30 minutes.

Serves 6 to 8.

Baked Tomatoes with Bel Paese®

Leeks with Bel Paese®

Leeks with Bel Paese®

This vegetable dish goes nicely with lightly-seasoned baked fillet of flounder or sole.

3 leeks
3 tablespoons butter
1 tablespoon olive oil
2 cups milk
4 oz. Bel Paese® cheese*, thinly sliced
  Pepper

*Remove wax coating and moist, white crust from cheese.

To prepare leeks: Remove tops to within 2 inches of bulb. Remove outer layer of bulb. Wash leeks thoroughly. Cut into large pieces.

In medium saucepan, melt butter over medium-low heat. Add oil, milk and leeks. Cover and cook until tender, 20 to 30 minutes. Drain thoroughly.

Preheat oven to 350°F. Butter 1-quart casserole. Place leeks in prepared casserole. Cover with slices of cheese. Bake until cheese is melted, 10 to 15 minutes. Sprinkle with pepper to taste. Serve immediately.

Serves 4.

Zucchini with Parmigiano-Reggiano

2 lbs. zucchini, cut lengthwise
  into ½-inch strips
½ cup melted butter
½ cup freshly grated
  Parmigiano-Reggiano

In Dutch oven, heat 1 inch water to boiling. Add zucchini. Return to boiling. Cover and reduce heat. Simmer until tender-crisp, about 5 minutes, stirring once. Drain.

Arrange zucchini on serving platter. Top with butter and cheese.

Serves 4.

Eggplant with Bel Paese® and Prosciutto

1 large eggplant, peeled and cut
    lengthwise into ½-inch slices
    Salt
¼ to ½ lb. thinly sliced Prosciutto
    or boiled ham
5 oz. Bel Paese® cheese*,
    cut into narrow strips
    Milk for dipping
    Flour for coating
    Egg for dipping
    Fine dry seasoned bread
    crumbs for coating
    Vegetable oil for frying
½ cup beef broth
    Freshly grated Parmigiano-
    Reggiano

*Remove wax coating and moist,
 white crust from cheese.

Preheat oven to 350°F. Butter
12 × 8-inch baking dish. Set aside.

Sprinkle eggplant slices with salt.
Let stand about 30 minutes.
Meanwhile, wrap 1 slice Prosciutto
around each strip of Bel Paese®.
Set aside.

Rinse eggplant with cold water.
Drain. Dry with paper towels. Dip
eggplant in milk, then roll in flour.
Dip in egg beaten with 1 teaspoon
milk per egg, then roll in bread
crumbs to coat.

In large skillet, heat ⅛ inch oil
over medium heat. Fry eggplant
until golden brown, turning once.
Drain on paper towels.

Line bottom of prepared baking
dish with eggplant slices. Place
Prosciutto rolls on top of eggplant.
Add beef broth. Sprinkle with
Parmigiano-Reggiano. Bake until
golden brown and Bel Paese® is
melted, about 10 minutes.

Serves 4.

Vegetable Market, Florence Italy.

Bel Paese® Eggplant

1 eggplant, peeled and cut
    lengthwise into ½-inch slices
    Salt
    Milk for dipping
    Flour for coating
    Extra virgin olive oil for frying
    Vegetable oil for frying
6 oz. Bel Paese® cheese*,
    thinly sliced
1 can (16 oz.) peeled or crushed
    tomatoes
    Freshly grated Grana Padano

*Remove wax coating and moist,
 white crust from cheese.

Sprinkle eggplant slices with salt.
Let stand about 30 minutes. Rinse
with cold water. Drain. Dry with
paper towels.

Preheat oven to 350°F. Butter
9-inch square baking dish. Set
aside. Dip eggplant in milk, then
roll in flour. In large skillet, heat
mixture of half olive oil and half
vegetable oil ⅛ inch deep over
medium heat. Fry eggplant until
golden brown, turning once.
Drain on paper towels. Place eggplant in prepared baking dish,
alternating with slices of Bel
Paese®. Cover with tomatoes.
Sprinkle with Grana Padano.
Bake until eggplant is tender,
about 30 minutes.

Serves 4 to 6.

Crispy Zucchini/Fontina Sandwiches

4 small zucchini, cut lengthwise
    into ¼-inch slices
4 oz. Fontina
1 egg, beaten
¾ to 1 cup fine dry bread crumbs
    Vegetable oil for frying

In large saucepan, heat water to
boiling. Add zucchini. Cook for 3
minutes. Drain. Cool on wire rack.

Cut Fontina into thin strips, the
same size and shape as zucchini.
Place cheese strip between slices
of zucchini to make a sandwich.
Press lightly together. Sandwiches
can be cut in half for easier handling. Dip sandwiches in egg, then
roll carefully in bread crumbs.

In large skillet, heat ⅛ inch oil
over medium heat. Fry zucchini
until golden brown, turning once.
Drain on paper towels. Serve
immediately.

Serves 4.

Cauliflower/Provolone Puff Pastry

Cauliflower/Provolone Puff Pastry

1 cup cut-up cauliflowerets
1 sheet frozen puff pastry
    (10×9½×⅛ inch), defrosted
½ cup shredded mild Provolone* (2 oz.)

*Remove wax coating from cheese.

Cook cauliflower in salted water until tender-crisp. Drain thoroughly. Set aside.

Preheat oven to 400°F. Lightly grease a baking sheet. Set aside.

Cut pastry into 4 squares. Place ¼ cup cauliflower in center of each square. Top with cheese. Fold each square in half diagonally to form turnover. Crimp edges carefully with fork tines to seal. Place on the prepared baking sheet. Bake until golden brown, 20 to 25 minutes.

Serves 2 to 4.

Artichokes with Bel Paese®

4 artichokes
5 lemon slices
4 to 5 quarts water
½ teaspoon salt
6 oz. Bel Paese® cheese*, cut into 8 thin slices
¼ teaspoon dried oregano leaves

*Remove wax coating and moist, white crust from cheese.

Remove and discard coarse outer leaves of artichokes. Cut off sharp tips of leaves. Cut off 1-inch slice from top of each artichoke. Tie 1 lemon slice around each artichoke base.

In Dutch oven, heat water to boiling. Add artichokes, salt and lemon slice. Cook uncovered over medium heat until base is tender, 25 to 35 minutes. Remove artichokes. Turn upside down to drain.

Preheat oven to 425°F. Grease 13×9-inch baking dish. Set aside.

Cut artichokes in half lengthwise. Remove choke and attached hairs with knife. Arrange artichokes in prepared baking dish. Top each artichoke half with a slice of cheese and oregano. Bake until cheese is melted, about 10 minutes.

Serves 4.

Cauliflower and Bel Paese®

1 head cauliflower
⅓ cup freshly grated Grana Padano
6 to 8 oz. Bel Paese® cheese*, cut into
    thin slices
2 tablespoons butter, cut into small pieces
2 to 3 tablespoons half-and-half
1 tablespoon minced fresh parsley
⅛ teaspoon pepper

*Remove wax coating and moist, white crust from cheese.

Cook cauliflower in salted water for 20 minutes. Drain and cool slightly.

Preheat oven to 350°F. Divide cauliflower into flowerets. Place in buttered 1½-quart casserole. Sprinkle with Grana Padano. Cover with Bel Paese® Add butter and half-and-half. Sprinkle with parsley and pepper. Bake until heated through and cheese melts, 5 to 10 minutes.

Serves 4.

Artichokes with Bel Paese®

Vegetable Pie

This vegetable pie can be served with broiled meat, crispy sausage or a fresh garden salad.

- 2 leeks, cut into pieces
- 2 tablespoons butter
- 2 large carrots, cut into ¼-inch slices
- ¾ cup fresh green beans, cut lengthwise in half
- 6 eggs
- ½ cup milk
- 1 tablespoon all-purpose flour
- ½ teaspoon salt
- ⅛ teaspoon pepper
- ½ cup freshly grated Parmigiano-Reggiano

Preheat oven to 350°F. Butter 9-inch square baking dish or 9-inch quiche pan. Set aside.

In medium saucepan, cook leeks in small amount of boiling water until tender, 15 to 30 minutes. Drain.

In large skillet, melt butter over medium heat. Add leeks, carrots and beans. Cook 5 minutes, or until carrots and beans are tender-crisp, stirring occasionally.

In large mixing bowl, beat eggs, milk, flour, salt, pepper and cheese. Stir in vegetables. Pour into prepared baking dish Bake until set, 15 to 20 minutes.

Serves 4.

Onions can be substituted for leeks, and peas can be substituted for green beans.

Macaroni and Vegetables with Provolone

5 tablespoons extra virgin olive oil
1 sweet yellow or green pepper, seeded and cut into thin strips
3 medium ripe tomatoes, seeded and cut into thin strips
1 small eggplant, peeled and cut into small cubes
1 clove garlic, minced
2 anchovy fillets, chopped
1 tablespoon capers
5 pitted black olives, cut into halves
5 fresh basil leaves, minced or 1 tablespoon dried basil leaves
12 oz. macaroni, mostaccioli or medium shells
2 tablespoons extra virgin olive oil
¼ cup grated sharp (aged) Provolone
½ teaspoon salt
　Pepper

In large skillet, heat 5 tablespoons olive oil over medium heat. Add pepper, tomatoes, eggplant, garlic and anchovies. Cook until light brown. Reduce heat to medium-low. Add capers, olives and basil. Cover and cook until vegetables are tender, 15 to 20 minutes, stirring occasionally.

Meanwhile, in large saucepan of boiling water, cook macaroni until "al dente," tender but still firm. Drain. Place in large serving bowl. Sprinkle with 2 tablespoons olive oil. Toss to coat. Add hot vegetables and cheese. Season with salt and pepper. Mix gently. Serve immediately.

Serves 4.

Provolone Shish Kebabs

8 oz. mild Provolone*, cut into
　16 1-inch cubes
　Milk for dipping
　Flour for coating
2 eggs, beaten
1 tablespoon milk
¼ teaspoon salt
⅛ teaspoon pepper

1 to 1½ cups fine dry
　bread crumbs
4 to 5 oz. smoked slab bacon,
　cut into 1-inch pieces
8 small mushrooms, cut
　lengthwise in half
　Vegetable oil for frying

*Remove wax coating from cheese.

Dip each cheese cube in milk, then roll in flour. In small bowl, blend eggs, 1 tablespoon milk, salt and pepper. Dip floured cubes in egg mixture, then roll carefully in bread crumbs. Place coated cheese cubes on wax paper-lined plate. Refrigerate at least 20 minutes.

Dip bacon and mushrooms in egg mixture, then roll in bread crumbs.

In large deep skillet, heat 1 inch oil to 350°F. Meanwhile, alternate cheese, bacon and mushrooms on eight 6-inch wooden skewers. Fry 2 kebabs at a time until golden brown, about 1 minute, turning once. Drain on paper towels. Repeat for remaining kebabs.

Serves 4.

Green pepper cut into 1-inch cubes or ½-inch slices of zucchini can be substituted for mushrooms.

Provolone Shish Kebabs

Zucchini with Fontina and Mozzarella

6 to 8 ripe tomatoes
2 cloves garlic, minced
2 tablespoons extra virgin olive oil
10 fresh basil leaves, minced or 2 teaspoons dried basil leaves
¼ teaspoon salt
⅛ teaspoon pepper
Vegetable oil for frying
3 medium zucchini, peeled and cut lengthwise into ¼-inch slices
1 cup shredded Fontina (about 4 oz.)
1 cup shredded Mozzarella (about 4 oz.)

To remove peel from tomatoes: Place tomatoes in boiling water for 30 to 60 seconds. Remove from water. Plunge tomatoes into cold water. Remove and discard peel and seeds. Chop tomato pulp.

In large skillet, sauté garlic in olive oil. Add tomatoes, basil, salt and pepper. Stir and cook until sauce thickens, 20 to 30 minutes.

Meanwhile, in medium skillet, heat ⅛ inch vegetable oil over medium heat. Fry zucchini until golden brown, turning once. Drain on paper towels. Preheat oven to 350°F. Arrange half the zucchini in 9-inch square baking dish. Cover with half the tomato sauce. Sprinkle with half the Fontina and half the Mozzarella. Repeat layers.

Bake until cheese melts, about 15 minutes or microwave at HIGH for 5 minutes, or until cheese melts.

Serves 4 as a main dish or 6 as a side dish.

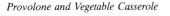

Provolone and Vegetable Casserole

Produce Market, Rome, Italy

Provolone and Vegetable Casserole

½ small head cauliflower, cut into flowerets
½ lb. broccoli
2 large carrots
1 potato, cut in half
½ fennel plant, cut up
1 clove garlic, minced
2 tablespoons butter
2 tablespoons all-purpose flour
½ teaspoon salt
1¼ cups milk
2 cups shredded mild Provolone* (8 oz.)
2 egg yolks, beaten
Pepper

*Remove wax coating from cheese.

Preheat oven to 350°F. Grease 2-quart casserole. Set aside.

In Dutch oven, cook vegetables in boiling water about 7 minutes. Drain. Cool and cut into small pieces. Arrange in prepared casserole. Sprinkle vegetables with garlic.

In small saucepan, melt butter. Stir in flour and salt. Blend in milk. Cook over medium-low heat until thick and bubbly, stirring constantly. Stir in cheese until melted. Remove from heat. Blend egg yolks into cheese sauce. Pour over vegetables. Sprinkle with pepper. Bake until hot, 20 to 25 minutes.

Serves 4 as a main dish or 6 as a side dish.

Baked Macaroni with Four Cheeses

¾ cup uncooked macaroni
1½ tablespoons butter
¼ cup freshly grated
    Grana Padano or
    Parmigiano-Reggiano
⅛ teaspoon ground nutmeg
¼ cup Mascarpone
¾ cup shredded Mozzarella
    (about 3½ oz.)
¾ cup shredded Bel Paese®
    cheese* (about 3½ oz.)
1½ tablespoons butter (optional)
¼ cup freshly grated
    Grana Padano or
    Parmigiano-Reggiano
⅛ teaspoon ground nutmeg

*Remove wax coating and moist, white crust from cheese.

Preheat oven to 350°F. Butter 1-quart casserole. Set aside.

In large saucepan of boiling water, cook macaroni until "al dente," tender but still firm. Drain in colander. Place in large mixing bowl. Stir in 1½ tablespoons butter, ¼ cup Grana Padano and ⅛ teaspoon nutmeg.

Spread a fourth of the macaroni mixture into prepared casserole. Spoon Mascarpone onto macaroni. Layer with a fourth of the macaroni. Top with Mozzarella. Add a third layer of macaroni. Sprinkle with Bel Paese®. Top with remaining macaroni. Dot with 1½ tablespoons butter. Sprinkle with ¼ cup Grana Padano and ⅛ teaspoon nutmeg. Bake until golden brown, about 20 minutes.

Serves 4.

Tagliatelle with Cream Sauce

Tagliatelle with Cream Sauce

7 to 8 oz. tagliatelle, cooked
    and drained
1 cup Mascarpone
1 pkg. (10 oz.) frozen peas,
    cooked and drained
2 oz. finely chopped Pancetta or
    Prosciutto (about ½ cup)
1½ cups shredded Mozzarella
    (about 6 oz.)
    Butter

Preheat oven to 350°F. Grease 9-inch square baking dish. Layer half the tagliatelle in prepared baking dish. Spoon half the Mascarpone onto tagliatelle. Sprinkle with half the peas and half the Pancetta. Top with half the Mozzarella. Repeat layers. Dot with butter. Bake until heated through, about 20 minutes.

Serves 4 to 6.

Spaghetti All'Amatriciana

6 slices bacon
3 cloves garlic, cut in halves
1 lb. spaghetti
6 egg yolks, each in
    separate bowl
¾ to 1 cup freshly grated
    Parmigiano-Reggiano

In medium skillet, fry bacon until crisp. Drain on paper towels. Crumble bacon. Set aside. Reserve 3 tablespoons bacon fat. Sauté garlic in reserved bacon fat. Discard garlic. Set aside bacon fat.

In large saucepan of boiling water, cook spaghetti until "al dente," tender but still firm. Drain in colander. Return to saucepan.

Add egg yolks, one at a time, to spaghetti. Stir vigorously. (The heat from the spaghetti will cook the egg yolks.) Stir in reserved bacon fat, bacon and grated Parmigiano-Reggiano. Mix well. Serve immediately.

Serves 4 as a main dish or 6 to 8 as a side dish.

Gorgonzola Ravioli

Gorgonzola Ravioli

Ravioli
3 to 4 cups semolina flour
5 large eggs, room temperature
½ cup lukewarm water
½ teaspoon salt
  All-purpose flour for rolling

Filling
5 oz. Gorgonzola
2 small zucchini (about 8 oz.)
  peeled and thinly sliced
2 tablespoons butter

Sauce
¼ cup butter
2 fresh basil leaves, torn into
  small pieces or ¼ teaspoon
  dried basil leaves
  Freshly grated
  Parmigiano-Reggiano

2 tablespoons freshly grated
  Parmigiano-Reggiano or
  Grana Padano
1 egg yolk
⅛ teaspoon ground nutmeg

For ravioli, on large wooden board, place 3 cups semolina flour. Make a well in center. In small mixing bowl, beat eggs. Blend in water and salt. Pour mixture into well. Mix with fingertips, working from edge of well toward edge of flour. Work dough together, adding more semolina flour as needed to make a stiff dough. Knead until smooth on board floured with all-purpose flour, about 5 to 10 minutes. Dough should be firm, but not crumbly. Divide dough into 3 flattened balls. Wrap in plastic wrap. Let rest at room temperature for 1 hour.

Allow Gorgonzola to soften at room temperature for 30 minutes. For filling, in small skillet, cook zucchini in butter over medium-low heat until soft, stirring occasionally. Drain thoroughly. In small mixing bowl, mash zucchini and Gorgonzola. Add Parmigiano-Reggiano, egg yolk and nutmeg. Mix well. Set aside.

To make ravioli, follow photo directions at right.

In Dutch oven, heat water to boiling. Cook ravioli a few at a time, until tender, 10 to 12 minutes. Remove with slotted spoon to warm platter. Repeat with remaining ravioli.

For sauce, in small saucepan, melt butter. Remove from heat. Stir in basil. Spoon sauce over ravioli. Serve with Parmigiano-Reggiano.

Serves 10 to 12.

Semolina flour is available in health food stores or in the specialty section of your supermarket.

**How to prepare
Gorgonzola Ravioli**

Place 1 ball of dough on lightly floured board. Roll out to ¹⁄₁₆-inch thick 16 × 20-inch rectangle. Cut dough into 2-inch strips. Place a scant teaspoon of filling at 2-inch intervals.

Moisten dough between mounds of filling and around edges with pastry brush dipped in water. Cover each filled strip of dough with a plain strip of dough. Press down lightly around filling.

Cut into 2-inch squares with pastry wheel or sharp knife. Seal edges with fork. Repeat with remaining dough and filling. As ravioli are sealed, place on floured surface in single layer.

Tortellini with Bel Paese®

2 tablespoons butter
4 oz. Bel Paese® cheese*, cut
  into small chunks
¾ cup heavy cream
3 oz. chopped Prosciutto
  (optional)
  Pepper
8 oz. tortellini

*Remove wax coating and moist,
white crust from cheese.

In small saucepan, melt butter.
Add cheese and cream. Cook over
low heat until smooth, stirring
constantly. Stir in Prosciutto.
Sprinkle with pepper to taste.
Remove from heat. Set aside.

In large saucepan of boiling water,
cook tortellini until "al dente,"
tender but still firm. Drain in
colander. Place in serving bowl.
Pour sauce over pasta. Toss to
coat. Serve immediately.

Serves 4.

Pasta with Mascarpone/Prosciutto Sauce

*Pasta with Mascarpone/Prosciutto Sauce
pictured on page 112*

½ cup butter
1 onion, minced
¼ lb. Prosciutto, chopped
1 lb. spaghetti or tagliatelle
4 cartons (100 grams each)
  Mascarpone
  Freshly grated Grana Padano
  or Parmigiano-Reggiano

In small skillet, melt butter over
medium heat. Add onion and
Prosciutto. Cook until onion is
tender. Set aside.

In large saucepan of boiling water,
cook spaghetti until "al dente,"
tender but still firm. Drain in
colander. Return to saucepan.
Quickly add Mascarpone. Mix
well. Add onion, Prosciutto and
butter. Toss to coat. Serve
immediately with Grana Padano.

Serves 4.

Tortellini with Bel Paese®

Spinach Pasta with Gorgonzola Sauce

4 oz. Gorgonzola
⅓ cup milk
3 tablespoons butter
⅓ cup heavy cream*
8 oz. spinach noodles or shells
⅓ cup freshly grated Parmigiano-Reggiano or
    Grana Padano
    Freshly grated Parmigiano-Reggiano

Allow Gorgonzola to soften at room temperature for 30 minutes.

In medium saucepan, combine Gorgonzola, milk and butter. Cook over low heat until smooth, stirring constantly. Add heavy cream. Cook over low heat, until hot and smooth, stirring constantly. Remove from heat.

In large saucepan of boiling water, cook pasta until "al dente," tender but still firm. Drain in colander. Place in serving bowl. Pour sauce over pasta. Toss to coat. Add ⅓ cup Parmigiano-Reggiano. Mix well. Serve with additional Parmigiano-Reggiano.

Serves 4.

* ⅔ cup half-and-half may be substituted for ⅓ cup heavy cream and ⅓ cup milk

Macaroni and Bel Paese®

2 tablespoons butter
2 tablespoons all-purpose flour
⅔ cup milk
7 to 8 oz. Bel Paese® cheese*, cut into small cubes
1 tablespoon freshly grated Pecorino Romano
⅛ teaspoon ground nutmeg
1 lb. macaroni

*Remove wax coating and moist, white crust from cheese.

In small saucepan, melt butter. Stir in flour. Blend in milk. Cook over medium-low heat until thick and bubbly, stirring constantly. Add Bel Paese®. Cook over low heat until cheese melts, stirring constantly. Add Pecorino Romano and nutmeg. Stir until smooth. Set aside.

In large saucepan of boiling water, cook macaroni until "al dente," tender but still firm. Drain in colander. Return to saucepan. Pour sauce over macaroni. Toss to coat. Cook over low heat until hot. Serve immediately.

Serves 4 as a main dish or 6 to 8 as a side dish.

Spinach Pasta with Gorgonzola Sauce

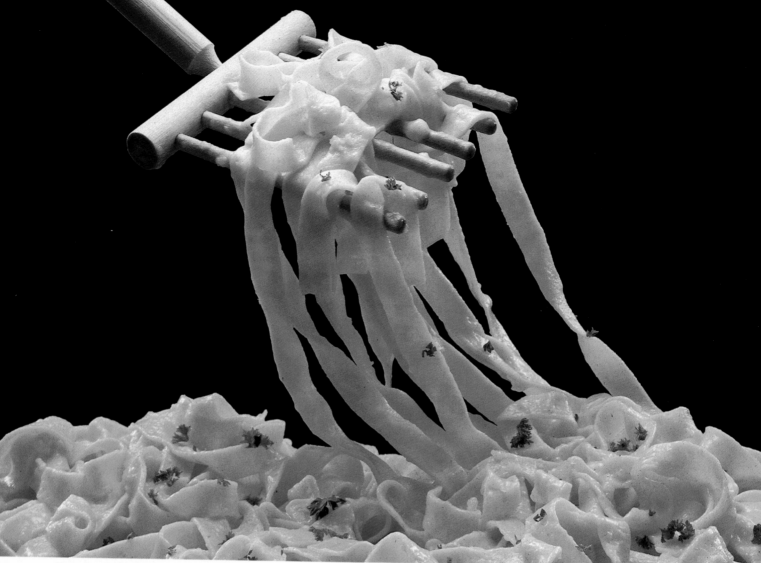

Fettuccini with Bel Paese®

Fettuccini with Bel Paese®

½ cup butter
2 oz. Bel Paese® cheese*, cut into small chunks
2 cups freshly grated Grana Padano (about 4 oz.)
1 cup heavy cream
1 lb. fettuccini or tagliatelle
2 tablespoons snipped fresh parsley
 Freshly ground pepper

*Remove wax coating and moist, white crust
 from cheese.

In small saucepan, melt butter. Add Bel Paese®.
Cook over medium heat until cheese melts, stirring
constantly. Reduce heat to medium-low. Stir in
Grana Padano and cream until smooth. Remove
from heat.

In large saucepan of boiling water, cook fettuccini
until "al dente," tender but still firm. Drain in
colander. Place in serving bowl. Add cheese sauce.
Toss to coat. Sprinkle with parsley. Season with
pepper. Serve immediately.

Serves 6 to 8.

Pasta with Bel Paese®

8 oz. Bel Paese® cheese*, cut into small chunks
1 cup half-and-half
½ teaspoon dried oregano leaves
2 egg yolks, beaten
1 lb. macaroni or spaghetti

*Remove wax coating and moist, white crust
 from cheese.

In top of double boiler over hot water, melt
Bel Paese®. Add half-and-half and oregano, stirring
constantly. Remove from heat. Add small amount
of cheese mixture to egg yolks, stirring until mixture
is smooth. Add back to cheese mixture, stirring
constantly.

In large saucepan of boiling water, cook pasta until
"al dente," tender but still firm. Drain in colander.
Return to saucepan. Add cheese sauce. Cook over
low heat until hot, stirring gently to coat pasta with
sauce. Serve immediately.

Serves 4 as a main dish or 6 to 8 as a side dish.

Baked Lasagna with Bel Paese® and Spinach

1 lb. fresh spinach
¼ lb. escarole or chicory
3 tablespoons freshly grated Parmigiano-Reggiano or Grana Padano
1 tablespoon butter, melted
1 teaspoon salt
¼ cup butter
¼ cup all-purpose flour
1½ cups milk
1 lb. lasagna noodles, cooked and drained
4 oz. Bel Paese® cheese*, thinly sliced
3 tablespoons freshly grated Parmigiano-Reggiano or Grana Padano
1 tablespoon butter, cut into small pieces

*Remove wax coating and moist, white crust from cheese.

Preheat oven to 350°F. Grease 13 × 9-inch baking dish. Set aside.

In large saucepan, cook spinach and escarole in boiling water until tender, 3 to 4 minutes. Drain well. Mince. Place in large mixing bowl. Stir in 3 tablespoons Parmigiano-Reggiano, 1 tablespoon melted butter and salt.

In small saucepan, melt ¼ cup butter. Stir in flour. Blend in milk. Cook over medium-low heat until thick and bubbly, stirring constantly. Remove from heat.

Alternate layers of noodles, spinach mixture and Bel Paese® in prepared baking dish. Top with sauce. Sprinkle with 3 tablespoons Parmigiano-Reggiano. Dot with 1 tablespoon butter. Bake for 30 minutes. Serve immediately.

Serves 6.

Lasagna with Bel Paese® with White and Red Sauces

Lasagna with Bel Paese® with White and Red Sauces

1 recipe Béchamel Sauce, page 66

Meat Sauce
½ medium onion, sliced
1 clove garlic, minced
2 to 3 tablespoons vegetable oil
1 lb. lean ground beef
1 can (28 oz.) crushed tomatoes or 1 can (28 oz.) whole tomatoes chopped
1 teaspoon dried basil leaves
½ cup thinly sliced celery
½ cup thinly sliced carrot

Lasagna Filling
1 lb. lasagna noodles, cooked and drained
6 oz. Bel Paese® cheese*, thinly sliced
6 hard-cooked eggs, sliced (optional)
2 tablespoons butter, cut into small pieces
1 cup freshly grated Parmigiano-Reggiano or Grana Padano (about 2 oz.)

*Remove wax coating and moist, white crust from cheese.

Prepare Béchamel sauce as directed. Set aside. Preheat oven to 350°F. Grease 13 × 9-inch baking dish. Set aside.

For sauce, in large skillet or Dutch oven, sauté onion and garlic in vegetable oil until tender. Add ground beef and cook until browned, stirring occasionally. Add tomatoes, basil, celery and carrot. Reduce heat to low. Cover and cook about 45 minutes. Remove cover and simmer 15 minutes.

Arrange a third of the lasagna noodles in bottom of prepared baking dish. Add half the Bel Paese® and half the eggs. Spread with meat sauce. Repeat layers of noodles, Bel Paese® and eggs. Spread with Béchamel Sauce. Top with layer of noodles. Dot with butter. Sprinkle with Parmigiano-Reggiano. Bake until golden brown, 30 to 40 minutes.

Serves 6.

Spaghetti alla Carbonara

4 slices bacon
4 egg yolks
⅛ teaspoon pepper
¼ cup heavy cream
½ cup freshly grated Pecorino Romano
7 to 8 oz. spaghetti
2 tablespoons butter, melted

In medium skillet, fry bacon over medium-low heat until crisp. Drain. Crumble bacon. Set aside.

In large mixing bowl, beat egg yolks and pepper. Stir in cream and Pecorino Romano. Set aside.

In large saucepan of boiling water, cook spaghetti until "al dente," tender but still firm. Drain in colander. Return to saucepan. Add egg mixture, bacon and butter. Cook over medium-low heat until egg is set, stirring constantly. Serve immediately.

Serves 2 as a main dish or 4 as a side dish.

Macaroni with Cauliflower, Raisins, Pine Nuts and Pecorino Romano

⅓ cup golden raisins
   Lukewarm water
1 small head cauliflower, cut into flowerets
3 tablespoons tomato paste
1½ cups hot water
1 medium onion, chopped
3 tablespoons vegetable oil
⅓ cup pine nuts
1 lb. macaroni
1 cup freshly grated Pecorino Romano
   (about 2 oz.)
   Fresh parsley sprigs (optional)

Place raisins in small bowl. Add lukewarm water to cover raisins. Let stand until raisins are softened, 10 to 15 minutes. Drain. Set aside.

Meanwhile, in medium saucepan, cook cauliflower in 1 inch boiling salted water until tender-crisp, 4 to 6 minutes. Drain. Rinse with cold water. Set aside. In small mixing bowl, dissolve tomato paste in hot water. Set aside.

In large skillet, sauté onion in vegetable oil until tender. Stir in tomato mixture. Simmer for 15 minutes. Stir in cauliflower, pine nuts and raisins. Simmer for 10 minutes.

In large saucepan of boiling water, cook macaroni until "al dente," tender but still firm. Drain in colander. Place in large serving dish. Pour sauce over macaroni. Toss to coat. Sprinkle with cheese. Garnish with parsley.

Serves 4.

Cannelloni

2 tablespoons butter
2 tablespoons all-purpose flour
1 cup milk
1 pkg. (10 oz.) frozen peas, cooked and drained or
   1 can (16 oz.) peas, drained
6 oz. Bel Paese® cheese*, cut into small chunks
¼ lb. fully cooked ham, cut into small chunks
8 to 10 cannelloni or manicotti, cooked and drained
   Freshly grated Parmigiano-Reggiano or
   Grana Padano
   Butter

*Remove wax coating and moist, white crust from cheese.

Preheat oven to 400°F. Grease 13×9-inch baking dish. Set aside.

In small saucepan, melt butter. Stir in flour. Blend in milk. Cook over medium-low heat until thick and bubbly, stirring constantly. Remove from heat. Reserve ⅓ cup for topping. Place remaining sauce in medium mixing bowl. Stir in peas, Bel Paese® and ham.

Gently fill each cannelloni with cheese mixture. Arrange in prepared baking dish. Spread reserved ⅓ cup sauce on cannelloni. Sprinkle with Parmigiano-Reggiano. Dot with butter. Bake until hot, 10 to 15 minutes.

Serves 4 to 6.

Spaghetti with Bacon and Pecorino Romano

8 or 9 slices bacon, chopped
1 onion, thinly sliced
1½ lbs. ripe tomatoes, peeled and chopped or 1 can
   (28 oz.) whole tomatoes, drained and chopped
   (reserve ⅓ cup juice)
1 teaspoon dried marjoram leaves
1 teaspoon pepper
1 lb. spaghetti
½ cup freshly grated Pecorino Romano

In large skillet, fry bacon until crisp. Add onion. Cook over low heat until tender. Add tomatoes, ⅓ cup reserved juice, marjoram and pepper. Cook over medium heat for 10 minutes, stirring occasionally.

In large saucepan of boiling water, cook spaghetti until "al dente," tender but still firm. Drain in colander. Place in large serving dish. Pour sauce over spaghetti. Toss to coat. Sprinkle with Pecorino Romano.

Serves 4.

Risotto

Risotto is a delicious northern Italian rice dish. It is extremely versatile — able to be served as a first course, main dish or dessert.

Instead of adding rice to boiling water and allowing it to simmer until the liquid is absorbed, as we do, rice for risotto is first fried in oil or butter for a few minutes until it is coated and translucent. Other ingredients may be added at this time. Liquid is then added in small amounts until the rice becomes chewy, but creamy. Almost constant stirring is required, but it is possible to sneak away for a few seconds at a time to look after the rest of the meal.

We have tried domestic rice in risotto dishes and while they were flavorful, the rice lacked the special creaminess that the Arborio rice imparts to risotto. Arborio rice is high in a special starch that dissolves into a creamy sauce while it cooks in liquid. This type of rice is also able to absorb a great deal of liquid and maintain its firmness. Arborio rice is available in gourmet sections of large department stores and in specialty food stores. The imported rice is, of course, more expensive but well worth the extra price.

Vialone rice or Canaroli rice are also recommended for risotto.

Risotto Milanese

Fontina/Parmigiano Risotto

4 to 5 cups chicken stock
⅓ cup chopped onion
3 tablespoons vegetable oil
1½ cups uncooked Arborio rice
½ cup Fontina, cut into small chunks (2 oz.)
½ cup freshly grated Parmigiano-Reggiano or
    Grana Padano (about 2 oz.)
½ teaspoon pepper
    Salt
2 tablespoon butter

In medium saucepan, heat stock to boiling. Reduce heat to simmer. Meanwhile, in large saucepan, sauté onion in vegetable oil over medium heat until onion is tender. Add rice. Cook until rice is well coated with oil, 2 to 3 minutes, stirring constantly.

Add ½ cup stock to rice. Cook until most of the stock is absorbed, stirring constantly. Add another ½ cup stock, and continue to cook, stirring constantly. Add more stock as it is absorbed. Cook and stir until rice is tender but firm, 20 to 25 minutes.

Stir in Fontina, Parmigiano-Reggiano and pepper. Season with salt. Cook 2 to 3 minutes longer, until sauce is creamy. Stir in butter. Serve immediately.

Serves 4 to 6.

Risotto Milanese

4 to 5 cups beef or chicken stock, broth or bouillon
⅓ cup minced onion
2 tablespoons diced Prosciutto
3 tablespoons extra virgin olive oil
1½ cups uncooked Arborio rice
1 cup dry white wine
¼ cup freshly grated Parmigiano-Reggiano
½ teaspoon pepper
    Salt
2 tablespoons butter

In medium saucepan, heat stock to boiling. Reduce heat to simmer. In large saucepan, sauté onion and Prosciutto in olive oil over medium heat, until onion is tender. Add rice. Cook about 5 minutes, stirring constantly. Slowly stir in wine. Cook until wine is absorbed, about 3 minutes, stirring constantly.

Add about ½ cup stock to rice mixture. Cook until most of the stock is absorbed, stirring constantly. Add another ½ cup stock. Add more stock as it is absorbed. Cook and stir until rice is tender but firm, 20 to 25 minutes.

Stir in cheese and pepper. Season with salt. Cook 2 to 3 minutes longer, until sauce is creamy. Stir in butter until melted. Serve immediately.

Serves 4 to 6.

Turban of Rice with Bel Paese®

Turban of Rice with Bel Paese®

¾ cup uncooked long-grain white rice
3½ to 4 cups boiling water
  5 oz. Bel Paese® cheese*, cut into small cubes
½ cup cooked peas
  1 egg, beaten
  3 tablespoons butter
½ cup cooked peas

*Remove wax coating and moist, white crust
from cheese.

Preheat oven to 350°F. Place shallow pan with water
1 inch deep on lowest oven rack. Generously butter
2- to 4-cup ovenproof ring mold. Set aside.

In medium saucepan, cook rice uncovered in boiling
water until chewy. Drain. Set aside.

In medium mixing bowl, combine cheese, ½ cup
peas, egg and butter. Add rice. Mix well. Pack
mixture into prepared mold. Bake until hot, 20 to 30
minutes. Let stand for 5 minutes. Loosen edges.
Carefully invert ring mold onto serving platter. Fill
center with remaining ½ cup peas to make a
"turban."

Serves 4.

Gorgonzola and Rice

  3 tablespoons butter
  2 cups uncooked long-grain white rice
  4 to 4½ cups beef stock, broth or bouillon
  2 oz. Gorgonzola
  3 tablespoons half-and-half
¼ cup freshly grated Parmigiano-Reggiano or
    Grana Padano
⅔ cup chopped walnuts (optional)

In medium saucepan, melt butter over medium heat.
Add rice. Cook until light golden, about 5 minutes,
stirring constantly. Slowly stir in stock. Heat to
boiling. Reduce heat. Cover and simmer until rice is
tender and stock is absorbed, 15 to 20 minutes.

In small saucepan, combine Gorgonzola and
half-and-half. Cook over low heat until Gorgonzola
melts and a thick sauce forms, stirring constantly. Stir
cheese sauce into rice. Remove from heat. Place in
serving bowl. Stir in Parmigiano-Reggiano. Sprinkle
with walnuts. Serve immediately.

Serves 4.

Mozzarella/Fontina Rice Quiche

1 small yellow onion, chopped
    or 1 leek, cut into
    small pieces
2 tablespoons butter
1 cup uncooked long-grain
    white rice
2½ cups beef stock, broth
    or bouillon
2 eggs
4 oz. Mozzarella, cut into
    small chunks
4 oz. Fontina, cut into
    small chunks
½ cup cooked, chopped spinach,
    well-drained
2 tablespoons minced
    fresh parsley
    Pepper
1 sheet frozen puff pastry
    (10 × 9½ × ⅛ inch), defrosted

Preheat oven to 425°F. Grease 9-inch round baking dish.

In medium saucepan, sauté onion in butter over medium heat, until tender. Add rice. Cook until light golden, about 5 minutes, stirring constantly. Slowly stir in stock. Heat to boiling. Reduce heat. Cover and simmer until stock is absorbed, 15 to 20 minutes. Remove from heat. Add eggs, one at a time, mixing vigorously. Add Mozzarella, Fontina, spinach and parsley. Season with pepper to taste. Mix well.

Line prepared baking dish with pastry. Trim off excess pastry. Spread cheese mixture into pastry. Place in oven. Reduce heat to 400°F. Bake until set and crust is browned, 30 to 40 minutes.

Serves 6.

Mozzarella/Fontina Rice Quiche

Rice and Cabbage with Bel Paese®

2 onions, sliced
1 tablespoon vegetable oil
1 cup thinly sliced Savoy cabbage
1 cup uncooked brown rice
1 cup dry red wine
1½ cups beef stock, broth or bouillon
½ cup water
5 to 6 oz. Bel Paese® cheese*, cut into small chunks
1 tablespoon freshly grated Pecorino Romano

*Remove wax coating and moist, white crust from cheese.

In large skillet, sauté onion in vegetable oil until tender. Stir in cabbage. Add rice, wine, stock and water. Heat to boiling. Reduce heat. Cover and simmer until almost all liquid is absorbed, about 50 minutes, stirring once. Add Bel Paese® and Pecorino Romano. Mix until Bel Paese® melts. Serve immediately.

Serves 4.

VARIATION: Substitute 1 cup uncooked long-grain white rice for brown rice. Reduce wine to ¾ cup. Reduce beef stock to 1¼ cups. Omit water. Simmer about 20 minutes.

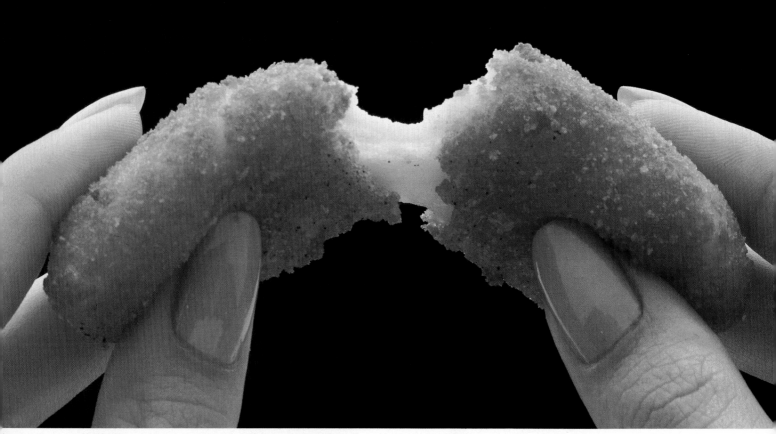

Bel Paese® Croquettes

Bel Paese® Croquettes

⅞ cup (¾ cup + 2 tablespoons) rice flour
2 tablespoons all-purpose flour
½ teaspoon salt
    Dash ground nutmeg
8 oz. Bel Paese® cheese*, cut into small pieces
½ cup milk
2 tablespoons butter
4 egg yolks, beaten
1 tablespoon milk
¾ cup fine dry bread crumbs
    Vegetable oil for frying

*Remove wax coating and moist, white crust from cheese.

In medium mixing bowl, combine rice flour, all-purpose flour, salt and nutmeg. Set aside.

In small saucepan, combine cheese, ½ cup milk and butter. Cook over medium-low heat, until cheese melts, stirring constantly. Add to flour mixture. Mix well. Refrigerate for 30 minutes.

Shape mixture into 3 × 1-inch croquettes. In shallow dish, blend egg yolks and 1 tablespoon milk. Dip croquettes in egg mixture, then roll in bread crumbs.

In large skillet, heat ¼ inch vegetable oil over medium-high heat. Fry croquettes a few at a time until golden brown, about 3 minutes, turning once. Drain on paper towels. Repeat for remaining croquettes.

Serves 4.

Rice flour is available in health food stores.

Parmigiano Rice Croquettes

1 cup uncooked long-grain white rice
2 cups milk
½ cup freshly grated Parmigiano-Reggiano
¼ teaspoon grated lemon peel
3 eggs, separated
    Vegetable oil for frying

In medium saucepan, combine rice and milk. Heat to boiling. Reduce heat. Cover and simmer until milk is absorbed, 15 to 20 minutes. Remove from heat. Stir in cheese and lemon peel. Cool.

Stir egg yolks into rice mixture. In small mixing bowl, beat egg whites at high speed of electric mixer until stiff. Fold egg whites into rice mixture.

In large skillet, heat ¼ inch vegetable oil over medium heat. Drop tablespoonfuls of rice mixture into hot oil. Fry croquettes a few at a time, until golden brown, turning once. Drain on paper towels. Repeat with remaining mixture.

Serves 4.

Gorgonzola Rice/Potato Balls

    2 medium potatoes
    1 cup uncooked long-grain
       white rice
4½ to 5 cups boiling water
    2 tablespoons butter
    2 eggs, beaten
    ½ cup seasoned bread crumbs
    ½ teaspoon salt
    2 tablespoons freshly grated
       Parmigiano-Reggiano or
       Grana Padano
    8 oz. Gorgonzola, cut
       into 16 pieces
       Flour for coating
       Vegetable oil for frying
       Fresh parsley sprigs (optional)

In small saucepan, cook potatoes
in boiling water until tender.
Drain. Cool slightly. Peel
potatoes. Press through sieve or
food mill, or mash until smooth.
In medium saucepan, cook rice in
4½ cups boiling water until chewy,
10 to 15 minutes. Drain.

In large mixing bowl, combine
potatoes, rice, butter, eggs, bread
crumbs, salt and Parmigiano-
Reggiano. Mix well. Shape about
⅓ cup mixture into a ball. Make a
hole in center of ball. Place piece
of Gorgonzola inside. Press potato
mixture over cheese to seal. Repeat.

Roll potato balls in flour. In
deep-fat fryer or deep saucepan,
heat 2 to 3 inches vegetable oil to
375°F. Fry potato balls a few at a
time, until golden brown, about 2
minutes. Drain on paper towels.
Place on serving plate garnished
with parsley.

Serves 4.

Gorgonzola Rice Potato Balls

POTATOES AND POLENTA

Cheese and Potato Pie

2 lbs. potatoes
½ teaspoon salt
¼ teaspoon pepper
7 oz. Gorgonzola, mild
    Provolone* or Caciotta,
    thinly sliced
6 tablespoons butter, cut into
    small pieces

*Remove wax coating from cheese.

In large saucepan, cook potatoes
in boiling water until tender.
Drain. Cool slightly. Peel potatoes. Press through sieve or food
mill, or mash until smooth. In
large mixing bowl, combine
potatoes with salt and pepper.
Mix well.

Preheat oven to 350°F. Butter
9-inch square baking dish. Spread
half the potatoes into prepared
baking dish. Cover with cheese
slices. Top with remaining
potatoes. Dot with butter. Bake
until lightly browned, 15 to 25
minutes. Serve immediately.

Serves 4.

Parmigiano-Reggiano Potatoes

2½ lbs. potatoes
3 cups freshly grated
    Parmigiano-Reggiano
    (about 6 oz.)
6 tablespoons butter, cut into
    small pieces
1 to 1¼ cups milk

Preheat oven to 350°F. Butter
12 × 8-inch baking dish. Peel and
slice potatoes. Arrange layers of
potato in prepared baking dish,
slightly overlapping. Sprinkle each
layer with cheese. Dot each layer
with butter. Pour milk over
potatoes. Bake until bubbly and
brown, 60 to 75 minutes.

Serves 4 to 6.

Potato Pancakes with Grated Italian Cheeses

Potato Pancakes with Grated Italian Cheeses

3 medium potatoes, peeled
    and shredded
1 cup freshly grated Caciotta or
    Toscanello (3 oz.)
¾ cup freshly grated Pecorino
    Romano or sharp (aged)
    Provolone (2 oz.)
2 eggs, beaten
¼ cup all-purpose flour
⅛ teaspoon pepper
⅓ cup vegetable oil

Preheat oven to 150°F.

In large mixing bowl, mix all
ingredients except vegetable oil.
In large skillet, heat vegetable oil
over medium heat. Drop 2 to 3
tablespoonfuls of batter into skillet
for each pancake. Fry pancakes 3
at a time, until brown, turning
once. Drain on paper towels.
Keep warm in oven until all pancakes are fried. Serve immediately.

Serves 4.

Potato Croquettes

2 lbs. potatoes
1 cup freshly grated
    Parmigiano-Reggiano
    (about 2 oz.)
2 eggs, beaten
2 tablespoons minced fresh
    parsley
¾ cup fine dry bread crumbs
    Vegetable oil for frying

In large saucepan, cook potatoes
in boiling water until tender.
Drain. Cool slightly. Peel
potatoes. Press through sieve or
food mill, or mash until smooth.

In large mixing bowl, combine
potatoes, cheese, eggs and parsley.
Mix well. Shape into 2 × 1-inch
croquettes. Roll in bread crumbs
to coat. Refrigerate 30 minutes.

In large skillet, heat ¼ inch vegetable oil over medium-high heat.
Fry croquettes a few at a time,
until golden, turning once. Drain
on paper towels.

Serves 4 to 6.

Potato Surprise

Potato Surprise

2½ lbs. potatoes
  3 tablespoons butter, melted
¼ cup freshly grated Parmigiano-Reggiano
  1 egg
  1 egg white
⅛ teaspoon salt
⅛ teaspoon ground nutmeg
  2 to 4 tablespoons fine dry bread crumbs

Filling
  8 oz. Mozzarella, cut into small chunks
¼ cup freshly grated sharp (aged) Provolone
¼ lb. Prosciutto, cut into small pieces

  2 tablespoons butter, cut into small pieces

In large saucepan, cook potatoes in boiling water until tender. Drain. Cool slightly. Peel potatoes. Press through sieve or food mill, or mash until smooth. In large mixing bowl, combine potatoes, 3 tablespoons butter, Parmigiano-Reggiano, egg, egg white, salt and nutmeg. Mix until smooth. Set aside.

Preheat oven to 350°F. Generously butter 9-inch round baking dish. Sprinkle with half the bread crumbs. Tilt dish to coat. Spread about half the potato mixture on bottom and sides of prepared baking dish.

In small mixing bowl, combine all filling ingredients. Sprinkle filling on potato mixture. Cover with remaining potato mixture. Sprinkle with remaining bread crumbs. Dot with 2 tablespoons butter. Bake until a thin crust forms, about 40 minutes. Let stand for 5 minutes. Invert baking dish onto serving plate, tapping gently to remove. Serve immediately.

Serves 4 to 6.

Potato and Cheese Casserole

1½ lbs. potatoes
  7 to 8 oz. Bel Paese® cheese*, cut into
    small pieces
⅔ cup milk
¼ cup heavy cream
  1 cup freshly grated Grana Padano (about 2 oz.)
¼ teaspoon salt
⅛ teaspoon ground nutmeg
¼ cup butter, cut into small pieces

*Remove wax coating and moist, white crust from cheese.

In large saucepan, cook potatoes in boiling water until tender. Drain. Set aside.

Preheat oven to 425°F. Butter 9-inch square baking dish. Set aside.

In small saucepan, combine Bel Paese®, milk and cream. Cook over medium-low heat, until cheese melts and sauce is creamy, stirring constantly.

Peel and slice potatoes. Arrange in prepared baking dish. Sprinkle with Grana Padano, salt and nutmeg. Pour cheese sauce evenly over potatoes. Dot with butter. Bake until hot, 15 to 20 minutes.

Serves 4.

Gorgonzola/Potato Casserole

3 to 4 oz. Gorgonzola
1 lb. potatoes
3 egg yolks, beaten

Allow Gorgonzola to soften at room temperature for 30 minutes.

In medium saucepan, cook potatoes in boiling water until tender. Drain. Cool slightly. Peel potatoes. Press through sieve or food mill, or mash until smooth. Set aside.

Preheat oven to 400°F. Lightly butter 1-quart casserole. Set aside.

In large mixing bowl, combine cheese and egg yolks. Mix with back of wooden spoon until smooth. Add potatoes. Mix well. Spread mixture into prepared casserole. Bake until hot, 10 to 15 minutes.

Serves 4.

Potato and Cheese Casserole

Gnocchi

Gnocchi (nyō´kē) are Italian dumplings made either of potato and flour or with flour alone. You can either make your own gnocchi "from scratch" following our recipe on the following page or buy them at the fresh pasta section in your supermarket. Frozen gnocchi are also available in the frozen food section of your supermarket. If you decide to make the gnocchi, allow yourself one and a half hours for cooking the potatoes and making the dough. Our recipe makes about three to three and a half pounds of gnocchi dough. If you do not want to use the dough all at once, you can freeze part of it or simply divide the recipes in half to reduce the amount.

Basic Gnocchi Dough

2½ lbs. potatoes	¾ teaspoon salt
2 cups all-purpose flour	¼ teaspoon pepper
2 eggs, beaten	Flour for coating
1 teaspoon baking powder	Serves 6 to 8.

Basic Gnocchi

How to Make Basic Gnocchi Dough

Cook potatoes in boiling water until tender. Drain. Cool slightly. Peel. Press through food mill or mash until smooth. In large mixing bowl, blend potatoes and remaining ingredients.

Mix dough gently with floured hands until it is no longer sticky. Shape a small amount of dough at a time into a roll ½ inch in diameter on a floured board. Cut rolled dough into 1-inch lengths.

Press dough with your thumb, against inside of fork tines. Roll toward end of fork. Coat with flour. Gnocchi will be cylindrical in shape.

Cook gnocchi a few at a time in boiling salted water until firm. Do not cover pan. Cooking time will depend on the size of gnocchi, but will be about 10 to 15 minutes.

Remove gnocchi from water with slotted spoon. Keep warm in 150°F. oven until all gnocchi are cooked. Top with melted butter or cheese before serving.

Bel Paese® Pastry Gnocchi

1 cup all-purpose flour
⅛ teaspoon salt
2 egg yolks
2 to 3 teaspoons water
5 tablespoons butter, cut into
   small pieces
1 cup shredded Bel Paese®
   cheese* (4 oz.)
¼ cup cooked spinach, thoroughly
   drained and minced
4 or 5 slices bacon, cooked and
   crumbled
3 tablespoons butter, melted
½ cup freshly grated Parmigiano-
   Reggiano or Grana Padano

*Remove wax coating and moist,
 white crust from cheese.

Sift flour and salt onto a board.
Make a well in center. In small
bowl, blend egg yolks and 2 teaspoons water. Add egg mixture
and 5 tablespoons butter to well.
Mix with fingertips until dough is
smooth, adding more water if
necessary. Shape into a ball.
Cover and refrigerate for 1 hour.

Blend Bel Paese®, spinach and
bacon into dough with fingertips.
If dough is too soft, refrigerate an
additional 30 minutes. Shape
dough into little balls. With your
thumb, gently flatten each against
inside curve of spoon.

Preheat oven to 375°F. Grease
9-inch square baking dish.

In large saucepan of boiling water,
cook gnocchi a few at a time, until
firm and cooked through, about
15 minutes. Remove with slotted
spoon. Drain. Place in prepared
baking dish. Drizzle with 3 tablespoons butter. Sprinkle with
Parmigiano-Reggiano. Bake for
5 minutes.

Serves 4.

Parmigiano Gnocchi

1 lb. potatoes
3½ cups all-purpose flour
¼ cup freshly grated
   Parmigiano-Reggiano
2 tablespoons butter, melted
2 eggs, beaten
1 teaspoon salt
⅛ teaspoon ground nutmeg
   Flour for coating
6 tablespoons butter
10 fresh sage leaves or ½
   teaspoon crushed sage
¾ cup freshly grated
   Parmigiano-Reggiano

In medium saucepan, cook potatoes in boiling water until tender.
Drain. Cool slightly. Peel potatoes. Press through sieve or food mill, or
mash until smooth. In large mixing bowl, combine potatoes, flour, ¼
cup Parmigiano-Reggiano, 2 tablespoons butter, eggs, salt and nutmeg.
Mix gently with floured hands to make a dough. Knead on floured
surface until firm, 3 to 5 minutes. Shape small amount of dough at a
time into ¼-inch rolls. Cut into 2-inch pieces. Roll gnocchi in flour to
lightly coat.

Preheat oven to 150°F. In large saucepan of boiling water, cook gnocchi
a few at a time until firm and cooked through, about 15 minutes.
Remove with slotted spoon. Drain. Place in 12 × 8-inch baking dish and
keep warm in oven until all gnocchi are cooked.

In small saucepan, melt 6 tablespoons butter. Stir in sage. Pour over
gnocchi. Sprinkle with ¾ cup Parmigiano-Reggiano.

Serves 8.

Parmigiano Gnocchi

Gnocchi with Fontina

1 recipe Basic Gnocchi Dough, page 134
8 oz. Fontina, thinly sliced

Preheat oven to 350°F. Grease 12 × 8-inch baking dish. Set aside. Prepare and shape Basic Gnocchi Dough as directed.

In large saucepan of gently boiling water, cook gnocchi a few at a time until firm and cooked through, 8 to 10 minutes. Remove with slotted spoon. Drain. Alternate layers of gnocchi and Fontina in prepared baking dish. Bake until cheese melts, 10 to 15 minutes.

Serves 6.

Gnocchi with Bel Paese®

¼ cup butter
10 fresh sage leaves or ½ teaspoon crushed sage
⅓ recipe Basic Gnocchi Dough, page 134
2 cups shredded Bel Paese® cheese* (8 oz.)

*Remove wax coating and moist, white crust from cheese.

Preheat oven to 350°F. Butter 9-inch square baking dish. Set aside.

In small saucepan, melt butter. Stir in sage. Set aside. Prepare and shape ⅓ Basic Gnocchi Dough as directed.

In large saucepan of gently boiling water, cook gnocchi a few at a time until firm and cooked through, 8 to 10 minutes. Remove with slotted spoon. Drain. Place in prepared baking dish. Drizzle with half the butter mixture. Sprinkle with half the cheese. Repeat layers. Bake until cheese melts, about 10 minutes.

Serves 4 as a main dish or 6 to 8 as a side dish.

Remaining ⅔ of dough can be shaped, cooked and frozen for future use.

Gnocchi with Bel Paese®

Bel Paese® Gnocchi with Spinach and Bacon

Spinach Gnocchi with Provolone

1½ lbs. potatoes
1½ lbs. fresh spinach
  1 cup shredded mild Provolone* (4 oz.)
  1 cup all-purpose flour
  1 teaspoon salt
  2 eggs, beaten
  4 oz. mild Provolone*, thinly sliced
    Freshly ground pepper

*Remove wax coating from cheese.

In large saucepan, cook potatoes in boiling water
until tender. Drain. Cool slightly. Peel potatoes.
Press through sieve or food mill, or mash until
smooth. Place potatoes in large mixing bowl.
Set aside.

Rinse spinach with water. Shake off excess. Place
spinach in large saucepan. Do not add more water.
Cover and cook over medium heat until tender, 2 to
3 minutes. Drain thoroughly. Mince spinach. Add
spinach and shredded Provolone to potatoes. Mix
well. Blend in flour, salt and eggs. Shape dough into
1-inch balls.

Preheat oven to 350°F. Grease 12 × 8-inch baking
dish. Set aside.

In large saucepan of gently boiling water, cook
gnocchi a few at a time until firm and cooked
through, 8 to 10 minutes. Remove with slotted
spoon. Drain. Place in prepared baking dish. Top
with Provolone slices and pepper. Bake until heated
through and cheese melts, 5 to 10 minutes.

Serves 4.

Bel Paese® Gnocchi with Spinach and Bacon

  1 recipe Basic Gnocchi Dough, page 134
  ½ lb. spinach, cooked, thoroughly drained
    and minced
  8 slices bacon, cooked and crumbled
1½ cups shredded Bel Paese® cheese* (6 oz.)
  ½ cup butter
  ½ to 1 cup freshly grated Parmigiano-Reggiano or
    Grana Padano (about 1 to 2 oz.)

*Remove wax coating and moist, white crust
 from cheese.

Prepare Basic Gnocchi Dough as directed *except* do
not shape. In large mixing bowl, combine Basic
Gnocchi Dough, spinach, bacon and Bel Paese®. Mix
well. Shape dough into little balls. With your thumb,
gently flatten each against inside curve of spoon.

Preheat oven to 150°F. In large saucepan of gently
boiling water, cook gnocchi a few at a time until firm
and cooked through, 8 to 10 minutes. Remove with
slotted spoon. Drain. Place in 12 × 8-inch baking dish
and keep warm in oven until all gnocchi are cooked.

In small saucepan, melt butter. Pour over gnocchi.
Sprinkle with Parmigiano-Reggiano.

Serves 4 as a main dish or 6 to 8 as a side dish.

Polenta

Polenta is a northern Italian specialty made of corn-meal served either hot or cold. Polenta is a hearty dish which may be eaten alone as bread or served with different sauces as a first course or combined with chicken, meat or cheese for the main course.

The dish originated in the late 1500's when corn (maize) arrived from the Levant. The Italians of Tuscany, Lombardy, Piedmont and Venetia made the maize into a thick, coarse, cornmeal mush. Many varieties of polenta can be prepared by combining cornmeal with all-purpose flour, semolina flour or buckwheat groats (kasha).

Preparing polenta "from scratch" is time-consuming because the cornmeal must be stirred frequently, if not continuously, for 30 to 40 minutes to keep lumps from forming and the cornmeal from sticking to the pan and burning.

For those occasions when time is of the essence, you can use an instant polenta which is available in specialty stores and Italian delicatessens.

Pecorino Romano with Polenta (Carbonara Style)

    9 slices bacon
    3 cloves garlic, each cut into several pieces

Polenta

    8 cups water
    1 teaspoon salt
2¼ cups yellow cornmeal

    4 teaspoons minced fresh parsley
    1 cup freshly grated Pecorino Romano
       (about 2 oz.)

In medium skillet, fry bacon until crisp. Drain on paper towels. Crumble bacon. Set aside. Reserve 2 tablespoons bacon fat. Sauté garlic in bacon fat. Discard garlic. Reserve bacon fat.

In Dutch oven, heat water and salt to boiling. Add cornmeal ½ cup at a time, stirring constantly with whisk to prevent lumps. Cook over medium heat, stirring constantly, until consistency of mashed pota-toes, 30 to 45 minutes.

Preheat oven to 400°F. Butter 12 × 8-inch baking dish. Spread half the hot polenta into prepared baking dish. Sprinkle with half the bacon and half the reserved bacon fat. Sprinkle with half the parsley and half the Pecorino Romano. Repeat layers. Bake until hot, 5 to 10 minutes.

Serves 6.

Northern Italy

Homemade Polenta

7½ cups water
1½ teaspoons salt
    3 cups yellow cornmeal
    5 to 6 tablespoons butter

In Dutch oven, heat water and salt to boiling. Add cornmeal ½ cup at a time, stirring constantly with whisk to prevent lumps. Cook over medium heat, stirring constantly, until the polenta is very thick and has the consistency of thick mashed potatoes, 30 to 45 minutes. Stir in butter until melted. Pour into 2-quart serving dish and pack down gently. Cool. Cut into slices.

Serves 6 to 8.

Polenta can also be spread into a 9 to 12-inch square on a wooden board.

Buckwheat Polenta with Bel Paese®

    4 cups water
1¼ cups butter, cut into small pieces
1¾ cups coarsley ground buckwheat groats (kasha)††
    8 oz. Bel Paese® cheese*, cut into small cubes

*Remove wax coating and moist, white crust from cheese.

In large saucepan, heat water and half the butter to boiling. Whisk in buckwheat groats. Cook over low heat until thickened, about 15 minutes, stirring frequently. Remove from heat. Add remaining butter and Bel Paese®. Cook over low heat until smooth and well blended, about 10 minutes, stirring con-stantly. Serve hot in soup bowls.

Serves 4.

††Do not use finely ground buckwheat pancake flour.

Pecorino Romano with Polenta (Carbonara Style)

Bel Paese®/Prosciutto Polenta

½ recipe Homemade Polenta, page 139
¼ cup freshly grated Parmigiano-Reggiano or
   Grana Padano
2 oz. Prosciutto, cut into small pieces
2 cups shredded Bel Paese® cheese* (8 oz.)

*Remove wax coating and moist, white crust
 from cheese.

Prepare Homemade Polenta as directed or prepare
instant polenta as directed on package. Spread into
8-inch square on wooden board. Cool.

Preheat oven to 350°F. Butter 9-inch square baking
dish. Set aside.

Cut polenta into ¼-inch slices. Arrange half the
polenta in prepared baking dish. Sprinkle with half
the Parmigiano-Reggiano, half the Prosciutto and
half the Bel Paese®. Repeat layers. Bake until cheese
melts, 15 to 20 minutes. Serve with a fresh garden
salad or with a side dish of vegetables.

Serves 4.

Polenta and Bel Paese® alla Longobarda

 1 recipe Homemade Polenta, page 139
1½ cups shredded Bel Paese® cheese (6 oz.)
 2 tablespoons all-purpose flour
⅛ teaspoon pepper
 1 cup milk
 1 egg yolk, beaten
12 slices bacon, cooked and drained

*Remove wax coating and moist, white crust
 from cheese.

Prepare Homemade Polenta as directed, except
spread into 8-inch square on wooden board. Cool.
Cut into ¼-inch slices. Arrange polenta in large
serving dish. Set aside.

In plastic bag, shake cheese and flour together to
coat cheese. In medium saucepan, combine cheese,
flour, pepper and milk. Cook over medium low heat
until mixture thickens and is creamy, stirring constantly. Remove from heat. Stir small amount of hot
mixture into egg yolk. Stir egg into hot mixture.
Cook an additional 1 to 2 minutes. Pour sauce over
polenta. Serve with bacon.

Serves 6.

Bel Paese®/Prosciutto Polenta

Bel Paese®/Mushroom Polenta

8 cups milk
1 bay leaf
½ teaspoon salt
1¼ cups yellow cornmeal
½ cup all-purpose flour
2 to 4 tablespoons butter
12 oz. fresh mushrooms, sliced or 3 cans (4 oz. each) sliced mushrooms, drained
½ teaspoon crushed sage
½ teaspoon dried rosemary leaves
1¼ cups shredded Bel Paese® cheese*, (5 oz.)

*Remove wax coating and moist, white crust from cheese.

In Dutch oven, heat milk, bay leaf and salt to a simmer. In small mixing bowl, blend cornmeal and flour. Whisk cornmeal mixture into milk mixture in a steady stream, stirring constantly to prevent lumps. Cook over medium low heat, stirring constantly, until the polenta is very thick and has the consistency of thick mashed potatoes, 45 to 60 minutes. Remove bay leaf. Spread into 9-inch square on wooden board. Let cool.

Preheat oven to 350°F. Butter 12 × 8-inch baking dish. Set aside.

Cut polenta into ¼-inch slices. Arrange half the polenta in prepared baking dish. Set aside. In large skillet, melt butter. Add mushrooms, sage and rosemary. Cook until mushrooms are tender. Remove from heat and drain.

Spread half the mushroom mixture on the polenta. Sprinkle with half the cheese. Repeat layers. Bake until heated through, about 30 minutes.

Serves 4 to 6.

Bel Paese®/Mushroom Polenta

Bel Paese® Baked Polenta

1½ oz. dried mushrooms or 1 can (4 oz.) sliced mushrooms, drained
⅓ recipe Homemade Polenta, page 139†
1 slice onion
2 tablespoons butter
¼ cup water
2 tablespoons butter
2 tablespoons all-purpose flour
¼ teaspoon salt
⅔ cup milk
½ cup freshly grated Parmigiano-Reggiano
2 cups shredded Bel Paese® cheese* (8 oz.)
1 tablespoons butter, cut into small pieces
¼ cup freshly grated Parmigiano-Reggiano

*Remove wax coating and moist, white crust from cheese.

If using dried mushrooms, soften by placing in bowl of warm water about 1 hour. Drain. Set aside. Prepare Homemade Polenta as directed, except spread into 8-inch square baking dish. Cool. Set aside.

In small saucepan, sauté onion in 2 tablespoons butter until tender. Stir in mushrooms and ¼ cup water. Cook over low heat about 20 minutes.

Meanwhile, in medium saucepan, melt 2 tablespoons butter. Stir in flour and salt. Blend in milk. Cook over medium low heat until thickened and bubbly, stirring constantly. Remove from heat. Add ½ cup Parmigiano-Reggiano and mushroom mixture.

Preheat oven to 450°F. Generously butter 9-inch square baking dish. Set aside.

Cut polenta into ¼-inch slices. Arrange half the polenta in prepared baking dish. Sprinkle with half the Bel Paese® and half the mushroom sauce. Repeat layers. Dot with 1 tablespoon butter. Sprinkle with ¼ cup Parmigiano-Reggiano. Bake until lightly browned, about 20 minutes.

Serves 4 to 6.

†Prepare ⅓ of recipe or prepare entire recipe and freeze unused portion for future use.

Polenta with Gorgonzola

Grilled Polenta with Parmigiano

1 recipe Homemade Polenta, page 139
   Vegetable oil for frying
½ to 1 cup freshly grated Parmigiano-Reggiano
   (1 to 2 oz.)

Prepare Homemade Polenta as directed, except spread into 12-inch square on wooden board. Cool. Cut into 6 × ½-inch strips.

Preheat oven to 375°F. In large skillet, heat 1/16 inch vegetable oil over medium high heat. Fry polenta strips until golden brown, turning once. Drain on paper towels.

Arrange fried polenta on baking sheet. Sprinkle with cheese. Bake until heated through, 5 to 10 minutes. Serve immediately.

Serves 6 to 8.

Polenta with Gorgonzola

4 cups water
½ teaspoon salt
2 cups yellow cornmeal
7 oz. Gorgonzola, thinly sliced
¼ lb. fully cooked ham, sliced
¼ cup milk

In large saucepan, heat water and salt to boiling. Add cornmeal ½ cup at a time, stirring constantly with whisk to prevent lumps. Cook over medium heat, stirring constantly until the polenta is very thick and has the consistency of thick mashed potatoes, 30 to 45 minutes. Pour into 2-quart serving dish and pack down gently. Cool.

Preheat oven to 350°F. Butter 9-inch square baking dish. Set aside.

Cut polenta into ¼-inch slices. Arrange half the polenta, a third of the Gorgonzola and half the ham in prepared baking dish. Repeat layers. Top with remaining cheese. Sprinkle with milk. Bake until cheese melts, 15 to 20 minutes. Serve immediately.

Serves 4.

Semolina Polenta with Pecorino and Salt Pork

½ lb. salt pork with rind, cut into small chunks
2 tablespoons extra virgin olive oil
1 large onion, thinly sliced
4 cups water
1½ cups coarsely ground semolina flour
½ cup thinly sliced pepperoni
⅔ cup freshly grated Pecorino Romano

In large saucepan, combine salt pork and olive oil. Cook over low heat until salt pork is reduced in size. Add onion. Cook until golden. Add water. Heat to boiling. Reduce heat to simmer. Cook for about 15 minutes.

Whisk semolina flour into water mixture. Add more water ¼ cup at a time, if needed. Cook over low heat until mixture thickens, about 20 minutes, stirring constantly. Add pepperoni. Mix well. Serve with Pecorino Romano.

Serves 4.

Polenta Gnocchi with Provolone

Sauce

- 8 oz. mild Provolone*, thinly sliced
- 2 cups milk
- 2 tablespoons all-purpose flour
- 2 egg yolks, beaten
- 1 teaspoon salt
- ¼ teaspoon pepper

Polenta

- 4 cups milk
- 4 cups water
- 1 tablespoon coarse salt
- 1¼ cups yellow cornmeal
- 2 cups shredded mild Provolone* (8 oz.)
- 3 to 4 fresh sage leaves, minced or ¼ teaspoon crushed sage
- 1 fresh rosemary sprig, minced or ½ teaspoon dried rosemary leaves

*Remove wax coating from cheese.

For sauce, in medium mixing bowl, soak sliced cheese in 2 cups milk about 1 hour.

Meanwhile, for polenta, in Dutch oven, heat 4 cups milk, water and 1 tablespoon salt to boiling. Add cornmeal ½ cup at a time, stirring constantly with whisk to prevent lumps. Cook over medium low heat until thickened and reduced, about 45 minutes, stirring constantly. Remove from heat. Add 2 cups shredded cheese. Stir until cheese melts and mixture is smooth. Spread polenta evenly into 15 × 10-inch jelly roll pan. Refrigerate for 30 minutes.

For sauce, remove ½ cup milk from cheese/milk mixture. Blend with flour in 1-cup measure. In medium saucepan, combine flour mixture, sliced cheese and remaining milk. Cook over medium low heat until mixture thickens and cheese melts, stirring constantly. Remove from heat. Stir small amount of hot mixture into egg yolks. Stir eggs into hot mixture. Cook an additional 1 to 2 minutes. Remove from heat. Stir in salt and pepper. Set aside.

Preheat oven to 350°F. Butter 12 × 8-inch baking dish. Cut cooled polenta into 2½-inch rounds with cookie cutter or sharp knife. Arrange polenta in prepared baking dish, overlapping edges. Sprinkle with sage and rosemary. Pour sauce over gnocchi. Bake until heated through and bubbly, about 25 minutes.

Serves 6.

Polenta Gnocchi with Provolone

Taleggio Polenta

- 4 cups water
- 1¼ cups butter, cut into small pieces
- 1½ cups coarsely ground buckwheat groats (kasha)††
- ½ cup yellow cornmeal
- 8 oz. Taleggio*, cut into small pieces

*Remove wax coating and moist, white crust from cheese.

In large saucepan, heat water and half the butter to boiling. In small mixing bowl, blend buckwheat groats and cornmeal. Whisk buckwheat mixture into water. Cook over low heat until thickened, about 15 minutes, stirring frequently. Remove from heat. Add remaining butter and Taleggio. Cook over low heat until smooth and well blended, 5 to 10 minutes, stirring constantly. Serve hot in soup bowls.

Serves 4.

††Do not use finely ground buckwheat pancake flour.

Veal Scaloppine with Red Wine

½ lb. veal cutlets
3 tablespoons butter or margarine
2 cups freshly grated Parmigiano-Reggiano or
    Grana Padano (about 4 oz.)
2 teaspoons all-purpose flour
3 tablespoons half-and-half
½ cup dry red wine
½ teaspoon salt
⅛ teaspoon pepper
1 tablespoon butter, melted
3 tablespoons fine dry bread crumbs

Preheat oven to 325°F. In large skillet, brown veal in
3 tablespoons butter over medium heat, turning
once. Remove veal. Place in 9-inch square baking
dish. Sprinkle with cheese. Set aside. Reserve
drippings in skillet.

In 1-cup measure, blend flour into half-and-half.
Add half-and-half mixture, wine, salt and pepper to
skillet. Cook over low heat until sauce thickens,
stirring constantly. Pour wine sauce over veal. In
small bowl, mix 1 tablespoon butter with bread
crumbs. Sprinkle over cheese. Bake until golden
brown and cheese melts, 20 to 25 minutes.

Serves 4.

Veal Chops with Bel Paese®

4 veal chops
3 tablespoons butter
¼ teaspoon crushed sage
¼ cup dry white wine
4 oz. Bel Paese® cheese*, cut into 4 slices
⅓ cup milk

*Remove wax coating and moist, white crust
 from cheese.

In large skillet, brown veal in butter and sage over
medium heat, turning occasionally. Add wine.
Reduce heat to medium low. Cook until wine is
reduced, about 15 minutes. Place Bel Paese® on
chops. Pour milk over chops. Cover and cook over
medium heat until cheese melts, 5 to 10 minutes.
Serve immediately.

Serves 4.

Veal Scaloppine with Red Wine

Atrani, Italy

Veal Cutlets with Bel Paese® Medallions

1 lb. veal cutlets
½ cup all-purpose flour
5 tablespoons butter
⅔ cup dry white wine
3 ripe tomatoes, peeled, seeded and chopped or
    1 can (16 oz.) whole tomatoes, drained
    and chopped
2 tablespoons butter
½ teaspoon dried oregano leaves
⅛ teaspoon salt
⅛ teaspoon pepper
2 (¾ oz. each) Bel Paese® Process Cheese
    Medallions, cut into small pieces
2 tablespoons hot water (optional)

Roll cutlets in flour to coat. In large skillet, brown
veal in 5 tablespoons butter over medium heat,
turning once. Add wine. Cook until mixture is
reduced and slightly thickened, about 5 minutes.
Add tomatoes, 2 tablespoons butter, oregano, salt
and pepper. Cover and cook over medium heat until
tomatoes are tender, stirring frequently, about 10
minutes. Remove cutlets from skillet. Place cutlets in
serving dish and keep warm.

Add cheese to tomato mixture in skillet. Cook over
medium heat, until cheese melts, stirring constantly.
Add hot water, if needed to thin sauce.

Spoon about 1 tablespoon sauce over each cutlet.
Serve with remaining sauce.

Serves 4.

Braciole (Beef Rolls) with Provolone

Braciole (Beef Rolls) with Provolone

This meat dish features braciole (brah chŏ′ lāy) with a cheese and bacon filling.

- 1 to 1¼ lbs. boneless beef round steak, cut into 4 equal pieces
- 2 cloves garlic, minced
- 4 oz. mild Provolone*, cut into strips
- 1 hard-cooked egg, peeled and sliced
- 2 teaspoons minced fresh parsley
- 4 slices bacon, cooked and drained (reserve bacon fat)
  Flour for coating
- 1 can (16 oz.) whole tomatoes, chopped
- ½ teaspoon dried basil leaves (optional)
- ½ teaspoon salt
- ¼ teaspoon pepper

*Remove wax coating from cheese.

Trim fat and pound beef into ¼-inch thickness. On each piece, place garlic, cheese, egg, parsley and bacon. Roll up each piece enclosing filling. Tie with string. Roll in flour to coat. Shake gently to remove excess flour.

In large skillet, brown beef in reserved bacon fat over medium high heat, turning occasionally. Add tomatoes, basil, salt and pepper. Heat to boiling. Reduce heat to low. Cover and cook until tender, about 1½ hours, occasionally adding water as needed. Remove string before serving. Serve with mashed potatoes.

Serves 4.

Rigatoni with Beef Stew

- 2 lbs. beef or veal stew meat, cut into ¾-inch pieces
- 1 tablespoon vegetable oil
- ½ cup chopped onion
- ½ cup dry white wine
- 1 can (28 oz.) whole tomatoes, chopped
- ½ to 1 teaspoon dried basil leaves
- 1 lb. rigatoni
- ½ cup freshly grated Pecorino Romano

In large skillet or Dutch oven, brown beef in vegetable oil over medium high heat, stirring occasionally. Add onion and sauté until tender. Add wine. Cover and cook over low heat, about 30 minutes, stirring occasionally. Add tomatoes and basil. Heat to boiling. Reduce heat to low. Cover and cook until beef is tender, about 2 hours.

In large saucepan of boiling water, cook rigatoni until "al dente," tender but still firm. Drain in colander. Place in large serving bowl. Add beef stew. Serve with Pecorino Romano.

Serves 6.

Stuffed Pork Braciole

- ¾ cup shredded Bel Paese® cheese* (about 3 oz.)
- 1 hard-cooked egg, peeled and minced
- 1 tablespoon freshly grated Parmigiano-Reggiano
- ½ teaspoon minced fresh garlic
- ½ teaspoon minced fresh parsley
- ½ teaspoon minced fresh basil
- 4 butterfly pork chops or 4 pork loin cutlets, ½ inch thick
- 4 thin slices Mortadella (about 3 oz.)
- 1 tablespoon dry Marsala

*Remove wax coating and moist, white crust from cheese.

Preheat oven to 350°F. In small mixing bowl, combine Bel Paese®, egg, Parmigiano-Reggiano, garlic, parsley and basil. Mix well. Set aside.

Pound chops to ¼-inch thickness. Place 1 slice Mortadella on each chop. Spoon about ¼ cup cheese mixture onto center of each slice of Mortadella. Carefully roll up each chop enclosing cheese mixture. Tie with string. Place in 9-inch square baking dish. Bake until pork is no longer pink, about 30 minutes. Sprinkle with Marsala during last 5 minutes of baking time. Remove string before serving.

Serves 4.

Meatballs Romano

4 slices bacon, chopped
1 onion, chopped
1 clove garlic, minced
1 lb. lean ground beef
1 cup freshly grated Pecorino
    Romano (about 2 oz.)
1 egg, beaten
1 teaspoon salt
⅛ teaspoon ground allspice
    Vegetable oil for frying
½ cup beef bouillon
½ cup dry white wine
1 teaspoon lemon juice
2 tablespoons minced
    fresh parsley
    Hot cooked pasta
    Freshly grated
    Pecorino Romano

In large skillet, fry bacon over medium low heat. Remove bacon. Set aside. Add onion and garlic to bacon fat. Cook until onion is tender. Remove onion and garlic with slotted spoon. Reserve bacon fat in skillet and set aside.

In medium mixing bowl, combine bacon, onion, garlic, ground beef, 1 cup Pecorino Romano, egg, salt and allspice. Mix well. Shape into 1-inch meatballs.

In large skillet, brown meatballs in reserved bacon fat and vegetable oil ⅛ inch deep over medium high heat, turning occasionally. Drain. Add bouillon, wine and lemon juice to meatballs. Heat to boiling. Reduce heat to medium. Cook until meatballs are cooked through and liquid is reduced by half. Sprinkle with parsley. Serve with cooked pasta and additional Pecorino Romano.

Serves 4.

Meatballs Romano

Chicken Cutlets Fontina

Chicken Cutlets Fontina

8 oz. fresh mushrooms, cut into slivers
2 tablespoons butter
4 boneless whole chicken breasts, split in half,
  skin removed
  Flour for coating
  Pepper
2 tablespoons butter
⅓ cup dry white wine
2 tablespoons Madeira or sherry
4 oz. Fontina, cut into 8 slices

Preheat oven to 350°F. In large skillet, sauté mushrooms in 2 tablespoons butter over medium heat until tender. Remove mushrooms. Set aside. Reserve liquid in skillet.

Roll chicken in flour to coat. Season with pepper. Add 2 tablespoons butter to skillet and brown chicken over medium heat, turning once. Remove chicken. Place in 9-inch square baking dish. Sprinkle with mushrooms. Set aside.

Add white wine and Madeira to skillet. Heat to boiling, stirring constantly. Reduce heat to low. Cook until liquid is reduced by half, about 5 minutes. Pour wine mixture over chicken. Bake until chicken is no longer pink, about 20 minutes. Place slice of cheese on each chicken breast. Bake until cheese is melted, about 5 minutes.

Serves 6 to 8.

Chicken Breasts or Turkey Cutlets with Parmigiano-Reggiano

4 boneless whole chicken breasts, skin removed or
  4 turkey cutlets, ½ inch thick
4 oz. Parmigiano-Reggiano, cut into 4 pieces
1 egg, beaten
  Flour for coating
2 tablespoons vegetable oil
1 tablespoon butter
1 tablespoon all-purpose flour
1 cup half-and-half

Pound each chicken breast to about ¼-inch thickness. Place 1 piece of cheese in center of each chicken breast. Fold in ends, then roll up enclosing cheese. Tie with string. Dip each chicken breast in egg, then roll in flour to coat.

In large deep skillet, brown chicken in vegetable oil and butter over medium high heat, turning once. Remove from heat. In 2-cup measure, blend flour into half-and-half. Pour over chicken. Cook until mixture begins to boil. Reduce heat to low. Cover and cook until chicken is no longer pink, 35 to 45 minutes. Remove string before serving.

Serves 4 to 6.

Turkey Cutlets with Bel Paese®

¾ to 1 lb. turkey cutlets
1 oz. Bel Paese® cheese*,
  chopped
1 oz. fully cooked ham, chopped
  (about ¼ cup)
1 tablespoon freshly grated
  Grana Padano or
  Parmigiano-Reggiano
1 tablespoon minced fresh
  mushrooms
  Salt
  Pepper
1 egg, beaten
  Flour for coating
2 tablespoons vegetable oil
¼ cup Marsala or red cooking
  wine
1 tablespoon all-purpose flour
¾ cup milk

*Remove wax coating and moist,
 white crust from cheese.

Pound each cutlet to about ⅛-inch
thickness. In small mixing bowl,
combine Bel Paese®, ham, Grana
Padano and mushrooms. Divide
mixture among cutlets. Place
mixture in center of each cutlet.
Fold in ends, then roll up
enclosing filling. Tie with string.
Season with salt and pepper. Dip
each cutlet in egg, then roll in
flour to coat.

In large skillet, brown turkey in
vegetable oil over medium high
heat, turning once. Remove from
heat. Remove turkey. Pour
Marsala into skillet. In 1-cup
measure blend 1 tablespoon flour
into milk. Add to skillet and stir.
Cook until mixture begins to boil.
Add turkey, reduce heat to
medium low and cover. Cook until
turkey is no longer pink, about 15
minutes. Remove string before
serving. Serve with sauce.

Serves 4.

Turkey Cutlets with Bel Paese®

Baked Chicken Parmigiano

  1 cup freshly grated Parmigiano-Reggiano
     (about 2 oz.)
  1 cup all-purpose flour
2½ to 3 lbs. broiler-fryer chicken, cut into pieces
  3 tablespoons butter or margarine
  2 tablespoons vegetable oil
  ½ cup dry white wine
  ¼ cup freshly grated Parmigiano-Reggiano

In medium mixing bowl, mix 1 cup Parmigiano-Reggiano and flour. Roll chicken in cheese mixture to coat. Shake gently to remove excess coating.

Preheat oven to 350°F. In large skillet, brown chicken in butter and vegetable oil over medium high heat, turning once. Place chicken in 13 × 9-inch baking dish. Pour wine over chicken. Sprinkle with ¼ cup Parmigiano-Reggiano. Bake chicken until juices run clear, 35 to 40 minutes.

Serves 4 to 6.

Chicken Breasts with Bel Paese® and Prosciutto

4 boneless whole chicken breasts, split in half,
  skin removed
2 eggs, beaten
  Fine dry bread crumbs for coating
  Vegetable oil for frying
2 oz. Prosciutto, chopped
4 oz. Bel Paese® cheese*, cut into 8 slices

*Remove wax coating and moist, white crust
 from cheese.

Preheat oven to 350°F. Dip chicken in egg, then roll
in bread crumbs to coat. In large skillet, brown
chicken in ⅛ inch vegetable oil over medium high
heat, turning occasionally. Place chicken in
12 × 8-inch baking dish. Bake for 20 minutes.
Sprinkle with Prosciutto. Place Bel Paese® on
chicken. Bake until chicken is no longer pink, 25
to 30 minutes.

Serves 6 to 8.

Chicken Breasts with Gorgonzola

½ cup all-purpose flour
½ teaspoon salt
⅛ teaspoon pepper
4 boneless white chicken breasts, split in half,
  skin removed
3 tablespoons butter or margarine
1 cup half-and-half
8 oz. Gorgonzola, cut into small pieces
1 tablespoon minced fresh parsley (optional)

In shallow bowl, combine flour, salt and pepper. Roll
chicken in flour mixture to coat.

In large skillet, brown chicken in butter over
medium heat, turning once. Reduce heat to low.
Add half-and-half. Cover and cook until chicken is
no longer pink, about 45 minutes. Place chicken in
serving dish and keep warm. Reserve sauce and
drippings in skillet.

Place Gorgonzola in medium saucepan. Add
reserved sauce and drippings. Cook over low heat
until Gorgonzola melts and sauce is creamy, stirring
constantly. Pour over chicken. Garnish with parsley.
Serve immediately.

Serves 6 to 8.

Tiramisú

Tiramisú (tē rah mē sú), a popular Italian dessert, means "pick me up"!

24 ladyfingers, split lengthwise
¾ cup espresso coffee, cooled
6 eggs, separated
6 tablespoons sugar
4 cartons (100 grams each) Mascarpone
2 tablespoons brandy
8 oz. bittersweet chocolate, chopped or
    coarsely grated

Preheat oven to 375°F. Arrange ladyfingers on baking sheet. Bake until toasted, 5 to 10 minutes. Arrange half the ladyfingers in 2 or 2½-quart oval or rectangular serving dish. Brush lightly with espresso.

In large mixing bowl, beat egg whites at high speed of electric mixer or with whisk until stiff. Set aside.

In small mixing bowl, beat egg yolks and sugar at medium speed of electric mixer until thick and lemon colored. Add Mascarpone and brandy. Stir gently. Gently fold egg whites into Mascarpone mixture. Spread half the mixture on ladyfingers in serving dish. Sprinkle with half the chocolate. Repeat layers of ladyfingers, espresso, Mascarpone mixture and chocolate. Cover with foil. Refrigerate at least 1 hour before serving.

Serves 12.

Chilled Mascarpone with Cognac

5 cartons (100 grams each) Mascarpone
½ cup sugar
4 eggs, separated
¼ to ½ cup cognac

In medium mixing bowl, blend Mascarpone and sugar. Add egg yolks, one at a time, stirring vigorously. Stir in cognac. Set aside.

In small mixing bowl, beat egg whites with whisk or at high speed of electric mixer until stiff. Gently fold egg whites into Mascarpone mixture. Spoon into dessert dishes. Refrigerate for 2 to 3 hours.

Serves 6 to 8.

Tiramisú

Mascarpone Graham Cracker Pies

Mascarpone Graham Cracker Pies

4 cartons (100 grams each) Mascarpone
2½ tablespoons all-purpose ground chocolate
2 small bananas, sliced
8 graham cracker tart shells (2-inch diameter)
24 semisweet chocolate chips or ¼ cup
    grated chocolate

In small mixing bowl, mix Mascarpone with ground chocolate. Place 2 or 3 banana slices in bottom of each tart shell. Divide Mascarpone mixture among tart shells. Garnish with banana slices and chocolate chips. Serve immediately.

Serves 8.

Finely grated semisweet or milk chocolate chips can be substituted for ground chocolate.

Mascarpone Fruit Salad

1 banana, sliced
1 Delicious apple, cored and cut into small chunks
1 pear, cored and cut into small chunks
1 orange, sectioned and cut into small chunks
1 can (8 oz.) pineapple chunks, drained
2 to 3 tablespoons fresh lemon juice
3 tablespoons sugar
2 to 4 tablespoons cognac

Cream Sauce
1 egg yolk
2 tablespoons sugar
1 carton (100 grams) Mascarpone

⅓ cup candied cherries or other fruit (optional)

In large mixing bowl, combine banana, apple, pear, orange and pineapple. Sprinkle with lemon juice, 3 tablespoons sugar and cognac. Mix gently. Cover and refrigerate about 1 hour.

Just before serving, prepare Cream Sauce. In small bowl, mix egg yolk and 2 tablespoons sugar. Add Mascarpone and stir until smooth. Gently stir Cream Sauce into fruit mixture. Spoon salad into serving bowl. Garnish with candied cherries.

Serves 4 to 6.

Peanut Butter and Mascarpone

For a nutritious between-meal snack or for an informal get-together, try this simple recipe.

1 cup Mascarpone
¼ cup peanut butter
   Crackers or unsalted wafers

In small bowl, blend Mascarpone and peanut butter. Spread on crackers to serve.

Serves 4 to 6.

Angelo's Delight

This chocolate cream delight is also fantastic spooned over fresh peach or nectarine slices.

2 cartons (100 grams each) Mascarpone
3 to 4 tablespoons all-purpose ground chocolate
2 tablespoons cognac or vermouth*
   Pound cake

In small mixing bowl, combine Mascarpone and chocolate. Stir vigorously until completely mixed. Add cognac and mix well. Serve over pound cake.

Serves 6 to 8.

Finely grated semisweet or milk chocolate chips can be substituted for ground chocolate.

*Milk can be substituted for cognac.

Amaretto Cookies and Mascarpone

2 eggs, separated
2 tablespoons sugar
2 cartons (100 grams each) Mascarpone
2 to 3 tablespoons rum, cognac or liqueur of
   your choice
12 to 16 amaretto cookies
¼ to ⅓ cup Marsala
2 to 4 tablespoons candied fruits or
   chocolate chips (optional)

In small mixing bowl, beat egg whites at high speed of electric mixer until stiff. Set aside.

In another small mixing bowl, beat egg yolks and sugar at medium speed of electric mixer until thick and lemon colored. Add Mascarpone and rum, mixing gently. Gently fold egg whites into Mascarpone mixture. Set aside.

Carefully dip each cookie in Marsala. Arrange 3 or 4 dipped cookies in each of 4 individual dessert dishes. Spoon Mascarpone topping over cookies. Sprinkle with candied fruits to garnish. Refrigerate for 1 hour before serving.

Serves 4.

Mascarpone Parfaits

4 cartons (100 grams each)
  Mascarpone
4 eggs, separated
1 tablespoon aspartame-sweetened
  powdered drink mix
4 to 6 sugar cookies

In small mixing bowl, blend
Mascarpone and egg yolks. Stir in
drink mix. Set aside.

In another small mixing bowl,
beat egg whites with whisk or at
high speed of electric mixer until
stiff peaks form. Gently fold egg
whites into Mascarpone mixture.

Crumble 1 cookie into each of 4
to 6 individual dessert dishes.
Spoon Mascarpone mixture onto
cookies. Refrigerate for 1 hour.

Serves 4 to 6.

Pears with Torta
Gorgonzola/Mascarpone

12 oz. Torta Gorgonzola/
  Mascarpone
12 d'Anjou or Bartlett pears,
  peeled and cored
1½ cups dry white wine
 1 cup sugar
¼ to ½ teaspoon ground
  cinnamon

Allow Torta Gorgonzola/
Mascarpone to soften at room
temperature for 15 minutes.
Meanwhile, cut pears crosswise
into 1-inch slices.

In Dutch oven, combine wine,
sugar and cinnamon. Add pear
slices. Stir to coat. Heat to
boiling. Boil about 5 minutes until
pears are tender, but not soft,
stirring frequently. Drain pears
and allow to cool.

Place Torta Gorgonzola/
Mascarpone in small mixing bowl.
Stir with wooden spoon until
smooth and creamy. Top pears
with cheese.

Serves 8 to 10.

Mascarpone Parfaits

Brandied Amaretto and Mascarpone

16 amaretto cookies
⅓ cup brandy
1 cup Mascarpone
5 eggs, separated
3 tablespoons sugar

In small bowl, soak 8 amaretto cookies in the brandy until brandy is absorbed.

In large mixing bowl, combine Mascarpone and egg yolks. Mix well. Stir in sugar. Add soaked amaretto cookies, one at a time, mixing well.

In medium mixing bowl, beat egg whites with whisk or at high speed of electric mixer until stiff. Gently fold egg whites into Mascarpone mixture. Spoon into 8 individual dessert dishes. Garnish with remaining cookies. Refrigerate at least 1 hour before serving.

Serves 8.

Children's Treat

2 cups Mascarpone
1 to 2 teaspoons cherry, grape or lime aspartame-sweetened powdered drink mix or 1 to 2 tablespoons cherry, grape or lime sugar-sweetened powdered drink mix

In small mixing bowl, blend Mascarpone and drink mix. Spoon into individual dessert dishes. Refrigerate about 30 minutes.

Serves 4 to 6.

Brandied Amaretto and Mascarpone

RECIPE INGREDIENT INDEX

Acknowledgments

I would like to acknowledge the help given to me by the Egidio Galbani Company, who furnished me with the majority of the recipes in this book which I have translated and adapted. I would also like to give credit to the various Italian Cheese Consortia for the information about their respective cheeses and for many of their recipes, which I have translated and adapted or developed into new recipes.

My thanks also to Mario Bogana for his technical assistance, and to Rose Chmura and Marilyn Hellmuth for their help in testing recipes. Last but not least, I would like to thank my office staff, who typed and retyped this manuscript.

Design by Cy DeCosse Incorporated, in collaboration with Bel Paese Sales Company, Incorporated.

Bel Paese, Galbani, and Dolcelatte are trademarks of Bel Paese Sales Co., Inc.

Editor: Myrna Shaw
Art Directors: Susan Schultz, William Nelson
Project Managers: Gail Bailey, Susan Kerston
Photographers: Stephen Holzemer, Tony Kubat, Jerry Robb
Food Stylists: Susan Zechmann, Susan Finley, Lynn Bachman